"Is it up to me to craft my life determined my story that lea sible that the story of my life could take a dramatic turn in another direction? These are the kinds of questions David Murray addresses in this inviting book, which serves as an invitation to discover all that we were created to be in the context of a far greater story."

Nancy Guthrie, author, *Even Better than Eden*

"*The StoryChanger* is a book about three characters and their stories. The first is a Scotsman named David Murray. I have known him for years, but until reading these pages I had no idea how his story was changed. The second character is anyone who picks up this book, reads it, and discovers how helpful it is to understand the story of their life written thus far. And the third character? Well, he's the StoryChanger— who is pretty aptly named. But I should leave it to David Murray to introduce you to him."

Sinclair Ferguson, Chancellor's Professor of Systematic Theology, Reformed Theological Seminary; Teaching Fellow, Ligonier Ministries

"Are you trying to make sense of your life or the lives around you? Are you looking for purpose? What matters? What matters the most? David Murray's *The StoryChanger* will give you answers and might even change your story. He writes as a man who understands people, but even more importantly, who understands God. Prepare to be encouraged and to see your life as part of a much grander and more important story than you can imagine."

Jason Helopoulos, Senior Pastor, University Reformed Church; author, *The Promise: The Amazing Story of Our Long-Awaited Savior*

"David Murray has given us a practical, accessible, and personal guide to show us how the Bible's big story transforms the stories of our lives. Jesus alone can change our stories—moving us from sadness to satisfaction, from loneliness to belonging, and from despair to hope. What a relief to know that we're part of a bigger story and that there's hope for us even after we've made a mess of life. I'm eager to see how this book will transform many people by introducing them to the divine author and StoryChanger we all need."

Drew Hunter, Teaching Pastor, Zionsville Fellowship, Zionsville, Indiana; author, *Made for Friendship*

"Can the story of my life be rewritten? If you or a friend is feeling trapped in a story that seems messy and meaningless, let David Murray introduce you to the StoryChanger who is rewriting the story of David's life and can do the same for you."

David Sunday, President, WordPartners; Teaching Pastor, New Covenant Bible Church, Saint Charles, Illinois

The StoryChanger

The StoryChanger

How God Rewrites Our Story
by Inviting Us into His

David Murray

WHEATON, ILLINOIS

Trade paperback ISBN: 978-1-4335-8085-7
ePub ISBN: 978-1-4335-8088-8
PDF ISBN: 978-1-4335-8086-4
Mobipocket ISBN: 978-1-4335-8087-1

Library of Congress Cataloging-in-Publication Data

Names: Murray, David, 1966 May 28– author.
Title: The storychanger : how God rewrites our story by inviting us into his / David Murray.
Description: Wheaton, Illinois : Crossway, 2022. | Includes bibliographical references and index.
Identifiers: LCCN 2021056101 (print) | LCCN 2021056102 (ebook) | ISBN 9781433580857 (trade paperback) | ISBN 9781433580864 (pdf) | ISBN 9781433580871 (mobipocket) | ISBN 9781433580888 (epub)
Subjects: LCSH: Storytelling—Religious aspects—Christianity. | Identity (Psychology)—Religious aspects—Christianity. | Change (Psychology) — Religious aspects—Christianity.
Classification: LCC BT83.78 .M88 2022 (print) | LCC BT83.78 (ebook) | DDC 242—dc23/eng/20220113
LC record available at https://lccn.loc.gov/2021056101
LC ebook record available at https://lccn.loc.gov/2021056102

Crossway is a publishing ministry of Good News Publishers.

VP		31	30	29	28	27	26	25	24	23	22
15	14	13	12	11	10	9	8	7	6	5	4	3	2	1

To my beloved congregation, First Byron CRC.
You have changed my story for the better and forever.

Contents

Introduction

If life is a story, is your life a good read? Is it a feel-good story or a tearjerker? Is it going according to plan, or is it out of control? Is your story going forward, backward, or round in circles? Is it exciting or boring? Wow or meh? Are you proud of your story or ashamed of it? Are you the hero of it or the villain in it? Will your story have a happy ending or a sad one? Are you writing your own story, or has someone else taken your pen? Are you wondering, "How do I change my story?"

If you're like most people, you're not happy with your story. You'd love to change parts of it or maybe rewrite the whole thing. Even if your story so far reads better than most, there are without a doubt painful chapters ahead that no amount of denial can delay. Perhaps you'll have chapters like "My Cancer" or "My Failed Marriage" or "My Disastrous Decision" or "My Addiction." At some point, we all ask, "How do I rewrite my story?"

If we do get through life with relatively few bad chapters, we still have to face the ultimate questions: How will my story end? Is this life all there is, or is there a sequel? If there's a sequel, how do I make sure it's a better story than this one? Is there a connection between my present life and my forever life? How do I rewrite my story both now and forever?

To change our story, we need the StoryChanger, Jesus Christ. By faith, we hand over our pen to the world's best-selling author, Jesus

Christ, and ask him to rewrite our story by inviting us into his Story. Then we'll get a story that was worth writing and a story that will be worth telling. Let's get to know the StoryChanger and how this amazing author can change our story with his Story.

Writing a new story begins with reading what we've written so far—even though it's often a difficult read.

1

Our Messy Stories

We can't go forward until we go backward. We can't write a new story until we've read our old one. "Why can't I just throw my old book away and start over? Why can't I just press *delete* then *open new document*?" Because we won't need or want to meet the StoryChanger until we accept *that* our stories need to be changed and admit *where* our stories need to be changed. If we don't read the story that got us to this point, we'll scrawl the same story of failure and frustration again and again.

It's not easy for many of us to confront our stories and be honest about them. That's why God's Story includes King Solomon's story. In the book of Ecclesiastes, Solomon demonstrates how to read and assess our story so that we will ask God for the new and better story that he wants to coauthor with us. Come and read Solomon's story with me, so our story can be changed by God's Story, just as Solomon's was. Then our story will end up in God's library of priceless books rather than in the bargain books dumpster.

Background

Solomon's story was a mixed story. When he lived for God, his story was great. When he left God out, his story went from bad to worse. We get both sides of his story in Ecclesiastes.

Thirty times in this book he describes a person living life "under the sun." That's the phrase Solomon uses to sum up his godless years. "Life under the sun" is a life lived only for the present and this world. It's a life that never looks above the here and now, never looks beyond this world's horizon. It's a life that's lost sight of the eternal and the heavenly above and beyond the sun. Pessimism and skepticism dominate these "under the sun" sections of his book.

But in thirteen other sections Solomon brings God into the story. There Solomon lives "above the sun." He sees beyond this planet, people, and time, and he sees God everywhere and in everything. Certainty, joy, and hope infuse these pages.

In Ecclesiastes 2:17–26, Solomon invites us to read, live, and feel the two contrasting sides of his story. It begins with a godless life (a life lived "under the sun"), but ends up with a God-centered life (a life lived "above the sun").

How did God rewrite Solomon's story? The same way he rewrites ours: by first helping us recognize and confess that our stories need to be rewritten.

Our Stories Need to Be Rewritten

Before we observe what makes our lives so messy and meaningless, we must remind ourselves that it wasn't always like this. As we'll discover in the next chapter, God originally made us to have good, meaningful, and purposeful stories with happy endings (Gen. 1–2). The first draft of world history and the human story was pristine perfect. But sin splattered ink all over the pages, and now no one's story lives up to God's ideal. Instead, as Solomon explains, our stories are sad, short, senseless, and stressful.

Our Stories Are Sad

Wherever he looked, Solomon saw sadness. "I hated life, because what is done under the sun was grievous to me" (Eccles. 2:17). Whatever he attempted left him more depressed than before. How much did he try, though? He tried everything. The first two chapters of his book describe his fanatical yet futile pursuit of satisfaction. He tried education (1:12–18), pleasure (2:1–3), success (2:4–17), and then work (2:18–23). His verdict on it all? Hatred of life because of the sadness of life. He tried everything in life, but everything left him tired of life.

Our Stories Are Short

Our stories are not only sad; they are also short. "All is vanity," Solomon concludes (Eccles. 2:17). The word *vanity* occurs thirty-eight times in Ecclesiastes, and means something short, transitory, and short-lived. It's used in the Bible for a breeze, a breath, or a vapor. That's what the longest and largest life amounts to—a short puff of wind. The book's opening words go even further: "Vanity of vanities! All is vanity," Solomon complains (not exactly the most appealing of opening sentences). "Vanity of vanities" was an ancient way of saying the shortest of the short, superlatively short (see Eccles. 1:2). Everything is so totally temporary and transient.

Our Stories Are Senseless

Solomon worked vigorously to find meaning in life, but without God in it, he couldn't see any sense to it or value in it. "For all is vanity and a striving after wind. I hated all my toil in which I toil under the sun, seeing that I must leave it to the man who will come after me, and who knows whether he will be wise or a fool? . . . This also is vanity and a great evil" (Eccles. 2:17–19, 21). What's really bugging him here is that everything he's worked for will eventually be handed over to someone else he doesn't know, someone of unknown character, someone who will probably fritter it all away without a thought for the person who worked so painfully for it in the first place.

"What's the point in that?" he asks. It's as irrational as trying to catch the wind. He despairs because there's no significance or meaning to it all. Nothing makes any sense to him (Eccles. 2:20). "Is this it?" he agonizes. No wonder he hates life under the sun. It's just foolish drudgery.

Our Stories Are Stressful

If you thought stress, insomnia, and work-life imbalance were just twenty-first-century problems, think again. Solomon was one of the elites, in the 1 percent, yet even for him, "all his days are full of sorrow, and his work is a vexation. Even in the night his heart does not rest. This also is vanity" (Eccles. 2:23). Work took a terrible toll on his body, mind, and soul. He was exhausted but couldn't sleep because of the stress. Smartphones and social media were still three thousand years away, but depression and anxiety were just as much a problem then as now.

This is life lived "under the sun," life lived from a purely human and worldly perspective. It writes stories that are sad, short, senseless, and stressful. Solomon was saying that if you want to hate life, live it without looking beyond it.

Changing Our Story with God's Story

"My story is sad." Does Solomon's story sound like your story? Can you relate to it? If, like Solomon, you confess to God that your story isn't turning out as you hoped, there is hope for you. Bring your story to God and say, "My story is not going well. It's sad, short, senseless, and stressful. Please change my sinful story, StoryChanger." You can't begin to imagine what kind of story he'll begin to write for you when you ask him to be the author of your life.

"My story will work out." Maybe you're still young and you think, "I'll be more successful than Solomon. I'm going to live life 'under the sun' but I'll be happy. I'll make it work." Don't waste your life. No one else has succeeded at this. Why do you think you'll be the exception? Don't give God just the last chapter (though he'll happily take that), but

right now give him every chapter you have left. He can write a much better life story for you than you ever could. And even if you fear you're near the end of your story, the StoryChanger can turn your painful life into a Pixar ending.

If you write your own story,
you'll write a tragic story.

So, if our stories need to be changed,
who can change them for good and forever?

God Rewrites Our Stories

Wouldn't you prefer a story that's happy instead of sad, endless instead of short, meaningful instead of meaningless, peaceful instead of stressful? The only way to get "above the sun," to get above the horizon of this world, is to bring God into our stories and install him at the center of our stories. God can change our stories with his Story. Solomon had been searching in vain for the "good" life, but instead of good he found only vanity. Although it does not come across in English translations, in the Hebrew text he mentions "good" four times. What's changed? God is now in the picture.

God Writes a Happy Story

After multiple verses of misery, joy shows up three times in Solomon's story: "There is nothing better for a person than that he should eat and drink and find enjoyment in his toil. This also, I saw, is from the hand of *God*. For apart from *him* who can eat or who can have enjoyment? For to the one who pleases *him God* has given wisdom and knowledge and joy" (Eccles. 2:24–26). What made the difference? What switched Solomon's sad story to a happy one? God.

God's name has appeared only once up to this point in Solomon's book, but now God's name shows up four times in just a few verses. We read "good" four times because we see *God* four times. Solomon is no longer looking at life from a human-centered perspective but from God's vantage point, and he concludes that God is the only source of joy. "For apart from him who can eat or who can have enjoyment?" (Eccles. 2:25).

God Writes a Meaningful Story

What made Solomon so happy? Did his life dramatically alter? No. It was still eating, drinking, working . . . eating, drinking, working. What changed was that he connected God with everything. "This [eating, drinking, working] also, I saw, is from the hand of God" (Eccles. 2:24). He traced everything to God's hand and spotted God in everything. He spied divine significance in the everyday and in the mundane. He was eating the same meals, drinking the same drinks, doing the same work as the "under-the-sunners," but he's now an "above-the-sunner" and therefore finds enormous joy in locating his big God in the small things. By relating everything to God, everything took on a whole new meaning and had a whole new value.

God Writes a Grace Story

Solomon didn't just see God in everything; he saw that God had graciously given him everything. "This also, I saw, is from the hand of God" (Eccles. 2:24). He had not earned it, but rather had been gifted it by God. Life was no longer about what he achieved, but what he received. He didn't have the power to give himself happiness; it was something given by God.

Solomon now took nothing for granted but considered everything as gifted: food, water, appetite, digestion, sight, hearing, smell, memory, health, sanity—all was from the gracious hand of God. God's grace was so astonishingly satisfying. It wasn't just material things that improved by grace; intellectual and spiritual things improved too. "For to the one who pleases him God has given wisdom and knowledge and joy" (Eccles. 2:26). Previously, Solomon's pursuit of wisdom and knowledge arrived at grief. But when God gave wisdom and knowledge, Solomon arrived at joy. All things were new. When our lives connect with God, we experience a new contentment with life. Heaven has begun on earth.

Changing Our Story with God's Story

Give the StoryChanger your book and your pen. Hand your story over to God and ask him to become your StoryChanger by becoming your StoryWriter. Jesus said, "I came that they might have life and have it abundantly" (John 10:10). Jesus came to change your story from one of death to one of life. If you ask him to change your story, the most common words will no longer be *I*, *me*, and *myself* but *God*, *God*, and *God*, because a God-centered life is a satisfying life. Pray, "Jesus, take the pen."

"I like my story so far." Maybe your godless story so far has been better than most, but have you read the ending? "To the sinner he [God] has given the business of gathering and collecting, only to give to one who pleases God. This also is vanity and a striving after wind" (Eccles. 2:26). No matter how hard you work to accumulate, you will leave empty; but those who live for God will inherit riches. Your epitaph will be "This also is vanity and a striving after wind." Theirs will be "God has given wisdom and knowledge and joy." Rewrite your story to rechisel your epitaph.

Jesus, though, offers even more than a happy *ending* through grace; he offers a happy *existence* through grace. Nothing gladdens like grace. Grace isn't just love for the undeserving; it's love for those who deserve anger. If a total stranger hands me a thousand dollars one day, I'm going home pretty happy. If someone I've stolen a thousand dollars from hands me a thousand dollars instead of punishing me for stealing a thousand dollars, I'm going home with a completely different kind of happy—a grace happiness, an off-the-scale happiness.

There's something about being gifted salvation when we deserve damnation that makes it far more enjoyable than an earned salvation. Most joys lose their initial energy, but grace-joy increases every day. Grace-joy jumps higher with age and, even when we die, we'll jump all the way into heaven's joys and never stop for all eternity. We won't need trampolines in heaven.

Do you want a happy-ever-after ending or a hell-ever-after unending?

Summary

Why can't I just press *delete* and *open new document*? Read your messy and meaningless story to see how much needs to be rewritten and what needs to be rewritten. You will find that you need the Story-Changer to rewrite your story.

How God Changed My Story with His Story

Although I was raised in a Christian home, I rejected my Christian upbringing in my teens and lived for money and pleasure. To outside observers, my life may have looked relatively moral, successful, and happy. But there were dark chapters in my past and dark habits in my present, and I knew there was a dark ending ahead. I tried hard not to think about my real story, preferring the fantasy version.

In my early twenties, my closest work colleague died of cancer in his thirties, and one of my bosses went to jail after killing a six-month-old baby in a car crash caused by his drunk driving. I saw that their stories could easily become mine. My story was already messy and meaningless, destructive and deadly.

I tried to rip some pages out, then whole chapters, but soon realized that I had to shred the whole thing and start over with a blank page. But how? How could I get rid of my past story? And even if I could wipe out the past and get a redo, how could I be sure I wouldn't write the same chapters all over again?

Seeing my growing depression, my mother gave me a Bible study book and urged me to read my Bible, which had lain unopened for years. Through reading God's Story over some weeks, I met the StoryChanger and saw how he could change my story for the better. God was offering to rewrite my story by inviting me into his. And he did.

Questions

1. How would you describe your story so far? What parts are you pleased with? What parts would you like to rewrite?

2. What makes you hate life? Or what would you say to someone who told you, "I hate life"?

3. How can you find more joy and satisfaction in everyday life and ordinary things?

4. How can you increase your enjoyment of God's mercy? How does being saved by mercy make someone happier than being saved by merit?

5. Take a piece of paper and write one-sentence descriptions of:

- Your past story
- Your present story
- Your future story
- Your forever story

Where do you need the StoryChanger to work first and most?

6. How has God changed your story so far?

Prayer

StoryChanger, I confess that my story is messy and meaningless. I hand my story over to you. Please rewrite it with your Story. Amen.

If our stories are messy and meaningless, how did they get that way? Was this how God made us? Not at all, quite the reverse, as we will now discover.

If we miss the beginning of a story, we'll miss the point of the story. Knowing how a story began helps us know where we are in the story and where it's going.

2

The First Story

Most stories begin with a happy, idyllic situation, before a villain appears and ruins everything. The middle of the story, and the majority of it, is about how the hero of the story fights the villain, reverses the ruin, and, at the end, returns to the original ideal—or even to a better one. That, in a nutshell, is the plot of *Star Wars*, *Harry Potter*, *Lord of the Rings*, and most other movies and books.

If that's the usual structure of a story, what will happen if we start reading it halfway through or start watching the movie an hour after it started? Without knowing how it began, we won't know what's going on, who's who, what's happened, what's wrong, or where the story is going. We'll be confused and disoriented, and probably give up on trying to figure out the plot.

That's where many of us are when it comes to the story of the world. We're living in the middle of the world's story, but we're confused and disoriented because we have no idea how the story began. Perhaps we haven't read chapter 1 and therefore don't know what's happened, who's who, what's gone wrong, what's going on, or where the story is going. The world is a bewildering and perplexing place for anyone who doesn't know how it began. So, how did the story of the world begin, and how does that impact our story for good?

Let's go back to the beginning of God's Story, to Genesis 1 and 2, to learn how the story of the world began. By doing so, we'll grasp not just God's ideal Story, but what's going on now and where and how God's Story will end. By figuring out the beginning, we'll get a better handle on the messy middle and uncover the route to a happy ending. Confusion, disorientation, and despair will be replaced with clarity, direction, and hope. And that will put us in a much better place to have God rewrite our story with his Story.

Background

God's Story of the world begins with the beginning of the world. The first chapter launches with "In the beginning, God created the heavens and the earth" (Gen. 1:1). It ends with "God saw everything that he had made, and behold, it was very good. And there was evening and there was morning, the sixth day" (1:31). It's a beautiful scene of an ideal world populated with ideal people. Let's take a closer look at both.

What did God's ideal world look like? It looked idyllic.

God's Story Begins with an Ideal World

Genesis 1–2 paints the world God made as full of bounty and beauty.

God Made a Bountiful World

When God made everything, he didn't just sprinkle a few samples of this and that here and there. He created an abundance of everything. He produced a plethora of planets, stars, and galaxies. He fashioned a profusion of animals, fish, and birds. He made a myriad of trees, plants, and herbs. He went big with land, sea, and sky. He multiplied elements, materials, chemicals, and crops. The world was full to the brim with the goodness and generosity of God. There was nothing tightfisted or miserly about the Creator's creation. No one could look at the first world and say God was a penny-pinching skinflint or a minimalist barbarian. Rather, the whole creation said

God was lavish and copious with gifts, teeming and overflowing with kindness.

God Made a Beautiful World

When God made the world, he didn't make just a functional world, but a beautiful world. "God saw everything that he had made, and behold, it was very good" (Gen. 1:31). It was so good that God took a whole day off from creating to study and enjoy his creation and invited us to join him in this celebratory rest (Gen. 2:1–3).

The universe didn't just work well; it awed deeply. Lovely landscapes, pretty petals, fresh flavors, super sights, amazing animals, flying fish, tall trees, and majestic mountains—all revealed the beautiful mind and character behind it all. In God's wonderful world, we gaze upon God's gorgeous wisdom, goodness, sovereignty, power, creativity, and glory. We see this in the macro and the micro, with the telescope and the microscope. Ugly wasn't just invisible; it was inconceivable. The beautiful world of Genesis 1–2 portrayed and presented a beautiful Creator.

Changing Our Story with God's Story

Praise God for his first story. It's an amazing first scene, isn't it? An ideal God delighting in his ideal world. We praise God as the origin of all species and the link that is now missing to many. We join with the whole creation in praising God for this glorious first chapter full of bounty and beauty. Given the perfect beginning of God's Story, we can tenaciously hope for a perfect ending.

Grieve over the ruined story. That first perfect scene now clashes noisily with the present painful scene. Instead of bounty and fullness, we see shortage and emptiness.

Instead of beauty and artistry, we see ugliness and disorder. We weep over our warped world. It's a sad scene and should produce a sad soul, because the end result is not just a ruined world but ruined souls. A villain came along and spoiled God's beautiful story. His name isn't the Joker, but the devil, and he's preparing to pounce in chapter 3 of Genesis and in the next chapter of this book.

Ask for a changed story. The fact that God's first story was so bountiful and beautiful gives us hope that what God did once, he can do again. Let's take our empty, ruined stories to Jesus the StoryChanger and ask that he would change our stories with his Story. He left the bounty and beauty of heaven to suffer emptiness and ugliness so that we can enjoy bounty and beauty again. Ask him to rewrite your story so that your ending will be like his beautiful beginning. Take your ugly void to Jesus and ask him to fill you with loveliness as only he can.

God's first world
forecasts God's final world.

What about the first people in God's
first world? They too were idyllic.

God's Story Begins with an Ideal People

However beautiful and bountiful the world was, the apex and climax of God's creation was humanity. Let's examine God's blueprint for humanity so that we know what's still possible in the future.

We Were Like God

God made humanity in his image. God said, "'Let us make man in our image, after our likeness. And let them have dominion over the fish of the sea and over the birds of the heavens and over the livestock and over all the earth and over every creeping thing that creeps on the earth.' So God created man in his own image, / in the image of God he created him; / male and female he created them" (Gen. 1:26–27).

This divine image God imprinted on humanity had six components:

- *Oneness:* Two different persons, male and female, equally imaging God together in perfect relationship.
- *Knowledge:* They knew everything they needed to know about their Creator and the creation.
- *Holiness:* They had holy hearts, minds, consciences, wills, desires, ambitions, emotions, and bodies.
- *Happiness:* Their greatest joy was that they were right with God and therefore friends with God.
- *Authority:* God gave them power over the creation and the creatures in it.
- *Work and rest:* Like God, they worked six days and rested one day.

Doesn't that make you envious? It's meant to! God wants us to look in this mirror and ask, "What happened?" Now, instead of oneness there's division; instead of knowledge there's ignorance; instead of holiness there's sinfulness; instead of happiness there's sadness; instead of authority there's anarchy; and instead of work and rest there's either all work or all rest, with few finding God's perfect 6:1 work-rest balance.

We Were with God

God walked with Adam and Eve and talked with them in ordinary everyday life. "They heard the sound of the Lord God walking in the garden in the cool of the day" (Gen. 3:8). This holy sound was their invitation to commune with God in God's garden. Their lives were centered upon and lived around God. They enjoyed sublime love, trust, and communication. God was with them and they were with God in the closest possible and happiest ever relationship. They were best of friends with one another and with God.

We Were for God

Our first parents found their deepest satisfaction and fulfillment in living not for themselves, or for one another, but for God. They dedicated themselves to serving and glorifying God in their daily callings and found God to be thoroughly thrilling. Serving God wasn't a drudgery or a duty but a delight. Humanity was never happier than when making God happy.

Changing Our Story with God's Story

Praise God for his first story. Does Genesis 1–2 not make you yearn for "the good old days"? Praise God for creating us like him, with him, and for him. Ideal people in an ideal world. Ask him to give you an idea of the ideal so that you know what ideal to aim for and ask for.

Grieve over the ruined story. We are no longer like God, with God, or for God. Instead, we're more like the villain, we live without God, and we are out for ourselves. What a mess we've inherited . . . and added to. We lament the wreckage. We oppose and resist the villain who's done so much damage and who's still ravaging our lives. We were made for God but now we make our own gods. The more we see the ideal, the more we see our idols, and the more we want to re-create the ideal.

Ask for a changed story. Do you not crave to be like God, with God, and for God? Our story may be far from God's ideal, but he has a great idea for how to return to the ideal. It's Jesus the StoryChanger who lived like God, with God, and for God so that we can live like God, with God, and for God. Ask him to change you by grace, to use his Story to rewrite your story. But, remember, no matter how much restoration we experience here, the final beautiful chapter is about ideal people thriving in an ideal world that's even more idyllic than Eden (see Rev. 22). We look back to the first ideal and we look forward to the final ideal because both sights give us an idea of the change we need and can have now through the ideal person, Jesus.

Jesus's Story was ruined
so that ours could be rewritten.

Summary

If God's Story launched with an ideal people in an ideal world, how does that impact our stories? *Know how God's Story began so that you'll want and write a much better middle and end.*

How God Changed My Story with His Story

When I restarted Bible reading in my early twenties, after many years of neglect, I began with the book of Joshua, because that's the Bible study my mother gave me. I found the first chapter particularly helpful because it repeatedly encouraged me not to fear as I commenced my journey out of the wilderness and toward God's promised land of heaven.

But after a few chapters of Joshua, I was totally lost and confused. "I need to go back to the beginning," I eventually figured out. So, I opened at Genesis and read chapters 1 and 2. There I read about the first days of the world's story, the first animals, the first humans, the first marriage, the first Sabbath, and the first work. Everything was so bountiful and beautiful in contrast to my messy and meaningless life. It made me long for what once was. And it still does. Going back to the beginning still helps me to know how I should live now, how much I need the StoryChanger for that, and what I have to look forward to in the new heavens and the new earth.

Questions

1. Give examples of when you've come in halfway through a story and how it confused you.

2. Where do you still see the remains of God's beauty and God's bounty in our world?

3. How can you use the story of God's ideal world to change your story?

4. Go through the six parts of God's original image in Adam and Eve (oneness, knowledge, etc.) and describe how different we are today.

5. How can you use the story of God's ideal people to change your story?

6. How does knowing the first brief chapters of God's Story change your view of the last endless chapter?

Prayer

StoryChanger, thank you for writing such a beautiful first chapter. Use your Story to reverse and rewrite my ruined story and give me confident hope of a happy ending. Amen.

So, what happened? How are things so bad when everything started so good? Prepare to meet the villain.

We can beat the story-shredder, if we believe he's beatable. If we don't believe he's beatable, we are already beaten.

3

The
Story-Shredder

Darth Vader, the Joker, the Sheriff of Nottingham, Gollum, Voldemort, Kylo Ren. What do all these characters have in common? They're all villains in famous stories. If there's no villain, there's no story.

The villain in the world's story is the devil, but he also wants to be the villain in our personal stories. He's been shredding stories for thousands of years, and he wants to add the shreds of your story to his incinerator. That's terrifying, isn't it? How can we stop that from happening?

If we can discover how the devil ruined the world's story, we can fend off his attempts to spoil ours. So, *how did the devil shred the world's story, and how do we keep him from shredding ours?* As we investigate Genesis 3, look out for some defensive strategies to use against him. If we know what he's like and how he operates, we'll have vital intelligence to safeguard ourselves and also enlist God's Superhero to beat him for us, so that our story will be read forever rather than shredded forever.

Background

In the previous chapter, we looked at the first story, full of beauty and bounty, harmony and unity, happiness and holiness.

In the chapter before that, we looked at our present messy and meaningless stories. This raises the question: What happened in between? How did we get from beautiful and bountiful stories to messy and meaningless stories? Something terrible happened, but what was it? A villain, whom we meet in Genesis 3, came on the scene.

How does this villain operate? His first strategy is telling us a false story.

The Villain Tells Us a False Story

The devil was originally a good and great angel. But despite his high position, he wanted the highest position, God's position. For this rebellion, he and many rebel angels with him were hurled out of heaven (Isa. 14:12–15; Ezek. 28:12–19; Rev. 12:9). Having failed to unseat God, the devil went on to attack humanity, God's image on earth, using one of God's creatures, a snake (Gen. 3:1). Through the snake, he attacked God's Story with a false story.

The Devil Doubts God's Story

The devil asked Eve, "Did God actually say, 'You shall not eat of any tree in the garden'?" (Gen. 3:1). This question changed the entire course of human history. "Did God really say that?" the devil needled. "Are you sure?" he asked. With this question, Satan planted the idea into Eve's mind that God's word is subject to human opinion, that it's up for debate. This one question mark spawned billions of doubts.

The Devil Distorts God's Story

God forbade eating from one tree, but Satan made it seem that God had prohibited *all* trees (Gen. 3:1). In doing so, he portrayed God as miserly and stingy. "He's stopping you from enjoying all the fruit trees? Why's he keeping so many good things from you?" Instead of stamping on the head of such a vile question and vicious questioner, Eve started a discussion, explaining that God had forbidden only one tree. But the damage was already done. By twisting God's prohibition and sowing suspicion about God's character, Satan had distorted Eve's thinking about God.

The Devil Denies God's Story

Having sown doubt about God's word and character, the devil then outrightly contradicted God's threat. "The serpent said to the woman, 'You will not surely die. For God knows that when you eat of it your eyes will be opened, and you will be like God, knowing good and evil'" (Gen. 3:4–5). The devil blatantly denied God's Story and then substituted it with his own. "God said you will die. But I say you will live as never before."

Changing Our Story with God's Story

Hate the devil. The devil is attempting to ruin your story with the same tactics he used to ruin the world's story. He doubts God's Story, distorts God's Story, and denies God's Story. So how should we respond? We should identify the devil as our greatest enemy, who is out to destroy us with false stories. He's still doubting, distorting, and denying God's Story. He's still replacing God's Story with his own. And his great aim is to ruin your story and my story. *Satan* means "adversary," and there's no worse adversary of God's people than Satan. So let's hate him with as much hatred as he hates us.

Defeat the devil. Follow Christ's example in Luke 4:1–13, where Jesus defeated the devil's doubts, distortions, and denials with God's Story. He didn't debate or discuss Satan's words; he quoted God's word. God's true Story is more powerful and persuasive than the devil's false story. So, get to know it, and use it in both defense and attack.

If you give the devil your pen,
he'll write you a horror story.

What will happen if we believe the devil's story? It will butcher our story.

The Villain Shreds Our Story

Our first parents chose to believe the devil's false story instead of God's true Story. They believed lies rather than truth. They *listened* to the devil's story, they *lusted* for forbidden pleasure, and they *longed* for independence from God (Gen. 3:6). The result was a ruined humanity and a ruined world (3:7–19).

Humanity Was Ruined

They were ashamed. Adam and Eve immediately lost their innocence. "The eyes of both were opened, and they knew that they were naked. And they sewed fig leaves together and made themselves loincloths" (Gen. 3:7). They felt awkward and uncomfortable with one another. Instead of openness there was hiding; instead of oneness there was two-ness; instead of transparency, there was opacity. They couldn't look one another in the eye.

They were afraid. When God came to walk with them in the garden, they "hid themselves from the presence of the LORD God among the trees of the garden" (Gen. 3:8). When he found them and asked why they were hiding, Adam replied "I heard the sound of you in the garden, and I was afraid, because I was naked, and I hid myself" (Gen. 3:10). God was now a terrible Judge to them rather than a loving

Father. His voice was no longer music to their ears, but a terror to their hearts. They ran *from* him, not to him.

They were alienated. Adam and Eve were alienated from God and alienated from one another. Their perfect marriage was now a perfect mess, as each began finger-pointing and blame-shifting (Gen. 3:11–13). But sin ruined more than their relationships.

The World Was Ruined

As a punishment for Adam and Eve's sin, God placed a curse upon the animals (Gen. 3:14), upon having and raising children (3:16), upon work and the environment (3:17–19), and upon life in general. Instead of life, bounty, and beauty, there was now death, decay, and disorder. Wherever the first humans looked, there was ruin.

Changing Our Story with God's Story

Weep over a ruined humanity. Sin has brought so much shame, fear, and discord into our relationships with ourselves, others, and God. Every time we add sin to our story, we generate additional pages of shame, fear, and discord. This is something to confess, weep over, and beg for help to avoid.

Weep over a ruined world. Every dead animal; every miscarriage, still-birth, or disabled child; every lost job, boring job, or unrewarding job; every hospital bed, surgery, disease, and death—all result from the villain's hatred for everything and everyone.

You'll never change your story until you weep over your story.

Is there any hope of overcoming the ruin?

God Rewrites Our Story

So, did God give up? Did he just throw the story away and abandon us? No, in the midst of the wreckage, God promised to reverse, redeem, and rewrite our stories. Genesis 3:14–15 shines a chink of bright light that kept God's people hoping throughout the Old Testament darkness. It contained the first gospel promise of a new Story.

The Devil Will Be Disgraced

Because the devil used the snake to ruin our stories, God put an extra curse on the snake to picture his judgment on the devil. In the supremely cursed snake, God supplied a model of his plan to destroy the devil (Gen. 3:14). The snake would now be thrown down on the ground and eat dust all its days, a biblical picture of evil's defeat that Adam and Eve would see every time they saw a snake.

The Devil Will Be Detested

Most snakes now hate humanity and most of humanity hates snakes. God put this enmity between humanity and snakes to picture the enmity he wants between humanity and the devil. Sin brought humanity into a "friendly" relationship with Satan, but God broke this newly formed alliance with the devil by turning humanity's friendship with Satan into hostility: "I will put enmity between you and the woman, / and between your offspring and her offspring" (Gen. 3:15). By putting such hostility between the devil and Adam and Eve, God restored them to friendship with himself. Enmity between people and the devil meant harmony between people and God.

The Devil Will Be Defeated

Though the snake can inflict the odd bite and even fatality upon humanity, in general, humanity has the upper hand. This fact in nature also signifies the defeat of the devil by God's grace and power. God promised a future seed, a Son descended from Eve, who would suffer nonfatal devil-inflicted wounds on his body, but who would ultimately and fatally crush the devil's head. God warned the devil of this coming Savior: "He shall bruise your head, and you shall bruise his heel" (Gen. 3:15). Whatever temporary pain the devil would inflict on the deliverer, the deliverer would ultimately triumph over the devil.

Changing Our Story with God's Story

Hope for humanity. God promises us a different ending to our story if we hand our story over to him for rewriting. All the stories God writes will end in total and complete victory. How will yours end? Here's the possibility of beginning a better story with a far better ending. You can make this possibility a certainty through faith in the devil-crusher (John 14:30; 1 John 3:8).

Hope for the world. Although God mandated a curse upon the world and everything in it, he also promised that through the Savior's victory over Satan, a new world will be created, full of beauty, bounty, and unity (Rev. 21). God, not the villain, will have the final victory (Rev. 22). The more we see the villain, the more we're thankful for our Superhero Savior, and the more confident we can be of a victorious life and a triumphant finale.

The serpent damages God's servant,
but God's servant destroys the serpent.

Summary

If the devil tells us a false story to ruin our story, whereas God can rewrite the worst story, how should we view the devil? *Know who the villain is and how he operates to defend yourself, defeat him with God's Story, and get your rewritten story into God's favorite books pile.*

How God Changed My Story with His Story

After reading the first two chapters of God's beautiful story in Genesis 1–2, I ventured into the darkness of Genesis 3. As a young Christian still confused about what God was doing in my life, I found it to be a clarifying chapter. It explained the story of my life up to that point by unmasking the villain and by exposing the lies he'd been telling me and I'd been believing.

The biggest and most influential lie the villain told me for twenty-two years was, "I want you to be happy and God wants you miserable." He did this primarily by painting a sinful life as a good life and a holy life as a grim life. I believed this lie, and it was ruining my life.

As I looked back on my life, I began to connect the devil's lies with my tears. For example, I remembered how what I expected to be one of my highest points became one of my lowest points. A few months before, I'd somehow managed to get an invite to a party that lots of the rich and famous would be attending. I thought I had really arrived when three highly acclaimed Scottish soccer players chatted with me in one visit to the men's bathroom. They'd just played in an international match, and they made me feel as if I were on the team with them.

One hour later, in the early hours of the morning, I was sitting outside on the steps of the club crying my eyes out as the "beautiful people" came and went. I was black-hole empty. Why? I didn't know the answer then, but as I read Genesis 3, I began to understand the connection between the devil's lies and my tears.

On those tear-stained steps, I reviewed my empty life and vowed, "No more. Never again." However, I didn't yet have a better story to replace the devil's. I remained in his grip listening to his ruinous lies. I could not defend myself, and I could not defeat him. I wanted a different story, but knew I couldn't write it myself, and I didn't know anyone else who could. Genesis 3 changed all that and began to change me for the better too. My sports heroes faded as Jesus emerged from Scripture as the Superhero who alone could beat the villain and rewrite my story.   .

Questions

1. What other villains can you think of? What can you learn from their characters, words, actions, and ends?

2. How has the devil doubted, distorted, and denied God's word in your life?

3. How can you hate the devil better and defeat the devil better?

4. How have you experienced shame, fear, and alienation as a result of sin?

5. What spiritual lessons can you learn from snakes?

6. How can the story of Genesis 3 change your story? How will you use this story to help change others' stories?

Prayer

StoryChanger, this villain is really scary. Be my Superhero by defending me, defeating him, and rewriting my story so that I share in your final and complete victory over him. Amen.

The StoryChanger sounds like the kind of successful author I need to work on my story. How do I hire him? Before we answer that question, we first need to heed his warning about failed authors who promise they can "help" us.

Failure can bring us closer to success. If we never fail at anything, we'll never succeed at anything.

4

The Failed Authors

Eighty-one percent of Americans feel that they have a book in them, and should write it. Of those who start to write, 97 percent never finish. Only one in five of the books submitted to publishers get published. Of the half million or so books published in the United States every year, the average sales are 250 copies each. By these measures, there are lots of disappointed authors in the United States![1]

But there are even more disappointed authors than the official stats reveal. We're all writing the stories of our lives, and we've all failed to write and publish the book we wanted. Some of us failed at the beginning, some of us fear failed endings, all of us have failed chapters. We're all failed authors, so we're all disillusioned authors.

And yet, no matter how bad and sad our story becomes, we're still reluctant to hand our pen over to a better author. Why? Because we still want to be the writers of our own story. The end result is

---

[1] Justine Tal Goldberg, "200 Million Americans Want to Publish Books, But Can They?," Publishing Perspectives, May 26, 2011, https://publishingperspectives.com/; Steven Piersanti, "The 10 Awful Truths about Book Publishing," Berrett-Koehler Publishers website, June 24, 2020, https://ideas.bkconnection.com/; Lorraine Santoli, "The Top Reason People Never Finish Writing Their Book," The Synergy Whisperer, October 20, 2015, https://thesynergyexpert.com/.

disappointing books, embarrassing books, tragic books, and horror books. How do we exchange our failed story for a better story?

John 4:1–42 reassures us that there is a way to a better story, to a story worth writing and publishing. It involves admitting that we're failed authors, avoiding the "help" of other failed authors, and then handing our keyboard to Jesus to retype our story and fill us with satisfying success rather than with hollow disappointment.

Background

One day, Jesus decided to leave Judea and head for Galilee, deliberately traveling through Samaria on the way. Why? He knew there was a failed author there whose story he was going to rewrite. When he arrived in Sychar of Samaria, he was tired, so he sat beside a well to refresh himself in the heat of the midday sun. That's when he sees Ms. Samaritan, the failed author he came to meet. Let's learn from her failures and Jesus's words so we can write a story of success.

How many of us are failed authors? All of us.

We Are All Failed Authors

One of Jesus's great skills was to get people to read their own stories, to get their manuscript out and face the reality of what they had written so far. That's what he did with Ms. Samaritan. Let's read what she had written up to this point.

A Story of Unquenched Thirst

It's no accident that Jesus "arranged" to meet Ms. Samaritan at a well in the desert, that their conversation centered around thirst and water, and that his first words to her were, "Give me a drink" (John 4:7). The scene is a picture of her whole life—a life of unquenched thirst, unfulfilled and unfulfilling desires, and drinking in pleasures that parched her soul into a desert.

That's why, after the initial interaction, Jesus said, "If you knew the gift of God, and who it is that is saying to you, 'Give me a drink,' you would have asked him, and he would have given you living water" (John 4:10). He was contrasting her striving life with his giving life. "You work, work, work for thirst, thirst, thirst. I give, give, give for life, life, life."

When Jesus said, "Everyone who drinks of this water will be thirsty again" (John 4:13), he wasn't referring primarily to the water in the well, but to the sins that had drained her life up to this point. He was saying, "You're only drinking deeper thirst." Her lifestyle was a deathstyle. Her drink was dust.

He therefore offers her another well of water, the satisfying spring of his salvation. "But whoever drinks of the water that I will give him will never be thirsty again. The water that I will give him will become in him a spring of water welling up to eternal life" (John 4:14). It's a remarkable offer: You can get an internal and eternal well, a well of satisfying refreshment inside you that will last forever.

That's an offer she can't refuse. Dropping her defenses, she says, "Sir, give me this water, so that I will not be thirsty or have to come here to draw water" (John 4:15). She's done with her soul-drying story and wants a revitalizing rewrite.

A Story of Hostile Prejudice

But there's more to this story than unquenched thirst. That's the main plot, but there are other subplots. For example, when Jesus first engaged her in conversation, she raised the long history of hatred and discrimination between the Jews and the Samaritans (John 4:9). Though evidently a big issue in her life, Jesus refuses to be distracted or diverted and turns the conversation back to his water (4:10). He knew that his water would wash away all bigotry and prejudice.

A Story of Sinful Spin

Ms. Samaritan asks for this water, but she's not yet thirsty enough to drink it. So, Jesus makes her uncover the secret story that had scorched her soul. "Jesus said to her, 'Go, call your husband, and come here.' The woman answered him, 'I have no husband.' Jesus said to her, 'You are right in saying, "I have no husband"; for you have had five husbands, and the one you now have is not your husband. What you have said is true'" (John 4:16–18). She told the truth, but not the whole truth. She told the truth in a way that told a lie. She was a skilled "spin doctor" but couldn't fool this spiritual doctor.

Five marriages and now a live-in boyfriend. She's on her sixth try for happiness in men. Each one promised satisfaction, but each one left her high and dry. Six dreams, six nightmares.

Changing Our Story with God's Story

What's your failed story? Where have you failed as an author? Where would Jesus take you in your story? How do you try to distract from your story? Face your story to face your failures.

How thirsty are you? How have you tried to quench your thirst? How many times have you attempted to turn your drought into a fountain? Ask the water of life to give you living water.

Failed authors
are thirsty authors.

I admit I'm not the greatest author, but other people have offered to rewrite my story. Should I let them?

Others Are Failed Authors

It's not only that we make a mess of our stories; others make a mess of our stories too. Some people want to impose their own story on our lives, and the culture subtly shapes our story too. If we allow either to happen, our stories are doomed, as Ms. Samaritan found to her cost.

Men Had Failed Her

In that culture, women did not initiate divorces. No matter how bad their marriages were, they stayed in them because they were entirely dependent upon their husbands. Men had all the power and all the resources. So, when we read of five divorces, we are reading a story of the serial abuse of a defenseless woman. They picked her up for a few brief pages of pleasure, then walked out of her story and forsook her. They took over her story, wrote their own on top of it, and then split. Each one promised her a better story, and each one wrecked her story. And now, the sixth, wouldn't even marry her. He just took from her and never gave himself to her.

The Culture Had Failed Her

The culture failed this woman in a number of ways. It allowed this kind of serial abuse of the weak. We can see how women were demeaned even in the disciples' reaction to her talking with Jesus (John 4:27). They also had absorbed a false cultural narrative about women that was far from the Bible's ennobling and elevating narrative for women. Jesus changed that narrative in his kind treatment of her.

The culture also had a false religious narrative that focused on traditional and external matters such as the place of worship (John 4:20). Again, Jesus switched the narrative by his answer that focused on the truth not tradition, and on the spiritual nature of worship not the physical place of worship (4:21–24).

Changing Our Story with God's Story

Don't let others write your story. Resist all other human authors and cultural forces who think they can write a better story for you. None of them are out for our ultimate good, and they will all fail as badly as we fail ourselves.

Change your worship to change your story. The climax of this water-and-thirst dialogue is worship. What we worship determines whether our stories will be satisfying and successful in the end. God wants us to worship him because we become like what we worship. If we worship God in spirit and truth, we'll become more spiritual and truthful. If we worship the well of spirit and truth, we'll be satisfied in our spirits with the truth.

*Change your worship
to change your story.*

I've failed, and others have failed. So, whom should I give my pen and paper to?

Jesus Is the Best Author

Jesus Changed the Woman's Story

"The woman said to him, 'I know that Messiah is coming (he who is called Christ). When he comes, he will tell us all things.' Jesus said to her, 'I who speak to you am he'" (John 4:25–26). We want the next line to be, "She believed him and gave her story over to him." Instead, the disciples gate-crash the climactic scene (4:27). This ends the conversation with Jesus, but it doesn't stop conversion to Jesus.

Her transformation is hinted at in the words "so the woman left her water jar" (John 4:28). The symbol of thirst, and failed attempts to quench it, is left behind. What was central to her life is now peripheral.

What she had focused on is now forgotten. That Jesus changed her story is even more clearly seen in her next words.

She Told Her Story

She left her water jar, went back into town, and said to the people, "Come, see a man who told me all that I ever did. Can this be the Christ?" (John 4:28–29). She left the town with a thirsty mouth but returned with a satisfied soul. She left a liar, but returned a truth-teller. She met the StoryChanger and wanted to tell her new story. The StoryChanger created a storyteller who herself became a storychanger.

Jesus Changed More Stories

"Many Samaritans from that town believed in him because of the woman's testimony, 'He told me all that I ever did'" (John 4:39). They asked him to stay and tell them more. For two days he heard their stories, told his story, and changed their stories with his (4:40–41). "They said to the woman, 'It is no longer because of what you said that we believe, for we have heard for ourselves, and we know that this is indeed the Savior of the world'" (4:42). One changed story changed many more stories.

Changing Our Story with God's Story

Has Jesus changed your story? How bad does your story need to get before you hand over your pen? Ask him to take over your story to blot out the sins of your past and to write a new story going forward. No story is so bad or so big that he can't rewrite it.

Has the StoryChanger made you a storyteller? Who needs to hear your story today? As Ms. Samaritan and the other

Samaritans tell us, our story is not about us, but it is all about the StoryChanger. The StoryChanger can change your story and make you a storyteller and a storychanger.

The StoryChanger
creates storytellers.

Summary

How do we exchange our failed story for a better story? *Admit we're failed authors, bypass all other aspiring writers, and ask Jesus to take the pen to write a satisfying and successful story.*

How God Changed My Story with His Story

When Jesus changed my story, I decided that one of the changes I needed to make was leaving my job in finance. It involved too much social drinking and also some low-level corruption. So, instead of giving my boss my six-monthly report, I gave him my resignation. He was not happy because he had invested a lot of time, money, and thought in preparing me for a position I had really wanted and recently had achieved. I offered him four-weeks' notice, but he said, "You can leave today. Give me your company car keys. Your salary ends today, as does your discounted mortgage" (4 percent at a time when interest rates were 12 percent!).

There I was, in my early twenties, with no job, no income, no home, and no car—and I was the happiest person in the world because I had Christ as my Savior. I knew he was writing a better story for me, even if I didn't know what it was at that point. I left my "water-pot" that had left me low and dry.

As I walked to the bus stop—jobless, penniless, carless, and soon-to-be houseless—I felt as if I had taken my failed story, turned to that day's page, written *The End*, and thrown it in the trash. I had no idea what the new book would look like. I had no idea what the first letter on the first page would be. But I knew a best-selling author was now author of my life and that he would write me the best story he could ever imagine for me.

Questions

1. How would you summarize your story so far? What are the chapter titles of your life?

2. Where have you failed as an author of your story?

3. What's your greatest thirst? How have you tried to satisfy that? What was the result?

4. How have others and the culture tried to write or influence your story?

5. Changing your worship changes your story. How so?

6. Who will you tell your rewritten story to this week?

Prayer

StoryChanger, I admit that no matter how hard I try, I am a failed author. Jesus, take the pen, change my story, and make me a storychanger.

I've failed to change my story. Others have failed
to change my story. Who can change my story, and
how? It's time to meet the StoryChanger.

The StoryChanger can change our unchangeable stories. Our stories cannot change until we meet the StoryChanger.

5

The StoryChanger

As the heaving self-help shelves on Amazon testify, transformation is one of the basic longings of the human heart. We want to be something better. We want to improve, progress, grow, and advance in one way or another. Most successful commercials, books, and movies appeal to this longing, as the hero not only overcomes difficulties and challenges to achieve his/her objective, but in the process becomes better, stronger, richer, kinder, or happier as a person. We love these "transformation" stories and dream of writing one for ourselves using the pen of education, fitness, fashion, health, psychology, politics, and many other big-promising change agents.

That's when we run into difficulty. We feel confused because we don't know what change for the better looks like. Or we feel frustrated because we don't know how to change for the better. Or we feel defeated because we've tried, failed, and given up trying to change for the better. Or we feel disappointed because we changed, but it didn't totally satisfy us.

Whatever our story up to this point has been, our stories have not changed as we would like. We need a StoryChanger. Is there a StoryChanger? *Who can change our story from stuck to transformed, and how does that happen?* No one's experienced or seen as much transformation as the apostle Paul and, in 1 Corinthians 6:9–11, he reveals the StoryChanger in a way that can change our stories too.

Background

First Corinthians is addressed to a divided church. Among the many causes of the divisions were Christians repeatedly taking other Christians to court for petty reasons and selfish gain (1 Cor. 6:1–8). The Corinthian story was becoming a story of damaging division, and therefore Paul attempted to unite them by their shared narrative of Christ-centered transformation. Instead of continuing to write a terrible story of division by their actions, Paul unites them by getting them to read their pre-StoryChanger story, which reads much like our own story, and then to compare it with their post-StoryChanger story.

What is our pre-StoryChanger story?

We Were Dirty and Damned

What was the Corinthians' pre-StoryChanger story? "Such were some of you," Paul says in 1 Corinthians 6:11. What were they?

They Were Dirty

Paul reminds the Corinthians about what they used to be. They were unrighteous, sexually immoral, idolaters, adulterers, homosexuals, thieves, greedy, drunkards, slanderers, and swindlers (1 Cor. 6:9–10). *Such were some of you.* The descriptions are self-explanatory, so let's just flag a few features of this list.

First, *"unrighteous" is separated from the rest of the list.* "Do you not know that the unrighteous will not inherit the kingdom of God?" (1 Cor. 6:9). Why does "unrighteous" come first and stand apart from the other descriptions on the list? Being unrighteous might not seem such a serious sin to us. But the "unrighteous" is someone who is not in a right relationship with God's law. God's law is not happy with the unrighteous and they are not happy with God's law. That is our root problem and the root sin of all other sins. It might not look as bad as the others, but it's actually the cause of all the others and, therefore, it's worse than all the others. If we are in a bad relationship with God's law, if we're not fully happy with God's law or God's law is not fully happy with us, then we're in the worst possible place and condition. That's worse than any of the actual sins that proceed from it.

Second, *idolatry comes between two kinds of sexual sin*, the first being sexual sin before marriage and the second being sexual sin within marriage. This unholy trinity tells us that idolatry births immorality and vice versa. A friend of mine who ministers to porn and sex addicts told me that he focuses most of his counsel on helping his counselees see that they need to deal with their self-idolatry if they are to stop their self-immorality.

Third, *the phrase "men who practice homosexuality" needs some care.* With this language, Paul implicitly distinguishes between same-sex attraction and same-sex practice. Both are sinful—as are illicitly heterosexual desires and practices outside of the marriage covenant—but doing it is more sinful than desiring it. Someone may have these desires but hate them, confess them, and fight against them by God's grace. That's very different from someone who has them, entertains them, cultivates them, and acts upon them. Both the attraction and the practice are part of our sinful nature (in the same way as heterosexual lust and practice), but the person who fights it by grace is going to heaven, whereas the one who practices it is not.

Fourth, *greed and gossip are on the same list as idolatry, immorality, and homosexuality.* Some use this fact to minimize the evil of immorality. But Paul's aim is to maximize the evil of greed and gossip, and all the other so-called "respectable sins." All sins are serious sins in God's eyes. All sins defile us. All sins dirty us.

They Were Damned

The Corinthians weren't just dirty; they were damned. Paul tells the Corinthians twice, "If you're on this sin list, you're on the no-heaven list." "Or do you not know that the unrighteous will not inherit the kingdom of God? Do not be deceived: neither the sexually immoral, nor idolaters, nor adulterers, nor men who practice homosexuality, nor thieves, nor the greedy, nor drunkards, nor revilers, nor swindlers will inherit the kingdom of God" (1 Cor. 6:9–10).

If you're unchanged and unchanging when you die, you won't be exchanging earth for heaven but earth for hell. Just like today, there were people telling the Corinthians the exact opposite. "Don't be ignorant and don't be deceived," warns Paul, "the dirty are damned, the lawless are lost, the unchanged are unsaved."

Changing Our Story with God's Story

"Such am I." If we're on this sin list, we're on the no-heaven list. These verses preview a notice on heaven's gates. It says to all who are on this sin list: No Entry! Many assure us that such sins are no longer sins or not serious sins. Paul calls such people *deceivers*. We cannot live like hell and go to heaven. We cannot reject God's law and get God's acceptance. We cannot choose grime and expect glory. We cannot reject kingdom law and still get kingdom life. We cannot live in sin and die in Christ. No repentance, no entry.

"Such was I." If we're off the no-heaven list and now on the no-hell list, we should rejoice. We run our finger down the list of sins and at various points, perhaps at all points, we say, "Such was I." We don't look down on those who are still on the sin list. We don't despise them. Even if we don't tick all the boxes now, we've ticked at least one of them in the past. We also know that if there's any unticked box, only God's grace explains that. We're not any better

than others. We got from "such am I" to "such was I" without any help from *I*.

You can't love filth
and love faith.

That's still my story. I'm still dirty and damned.
How do I change that? You need the StoryChanger.

We Are Spotless and Saved

We're about to examine the greatest revolution in world history. It's bigger than the religious revolution of the 1600s, the industrial revolution of the 1800s, the digital revolution of the late 1900s, or the identity revolution we're living through. It's a personal spiritual revolution. "And such were some of you. But you were washed, you were sanctified, you were justified in the name of the Lord Jesus Christ and by the Spirit of our God" (1 Cor. 6:11). "You were that, but you are now this." The contrast is intensified with three *buts* (these three *buts* are in the Greek text but not all are translated in the English text): "But you were *washed*, [but] you were *sanctified*, [but] you were *justified*." Let's look at how big these big words are to see how big a change this is. Each word gives a different perspective on the same change.

But you were washed. These phrases are all written in the passive voice, which means that this phrase could also be translated as "You've had yourselves washed." The Corinthians did not wash themselves; an outside party washed them. They were active sinners, but were completely passive in this massive washing. A spiritual Tide pod was dropped into their hearts and started a deep clean from deep within.

But you were sanctified. If we think of *washed* as God putting some-thing clean inside of us, then *sanctified* describes God separating us from the dirty dishes' side of the sink and putting us on the clean dishes' side. Just as God sanctified cups by separating them from common everyday use and dedicating them for holy uses in the Old Testament temple (Num. 7:1), so God separates his people from the dirty and damned side and dedicates us to the spotless and saved side.

But you were justified. Being washed starts the cleansing, but much dirt remains. Being sanctified sets us apart from the dirt, but we can still return to the dark side sometimes. Both washing and sanctifying are imperfect and ongoing. They are big changes, but not the biggest change. The biggest change is being justified.

Another way of putting this is *you were reformatted.* Anyone who uses a computer to type documents knows that the default format is words aligned to the left margin. But this leaves a jagged edge on the right of the page as each line comes up short to some degree or another. That can quickly be fixed by clicking the *justify* button, which lines up what we've written with both the left and right margins.

If the right margin is God's law, every line of every human life comes up short to one degree or another. But Christ can change all that quicker than a click when someone believes in him. Just as a click justifies jagged text immediately, so Christ justifies believing souls immediately. But, unlike computer formatting, Christ's formatting can never be changed back. Once *justified* is clicked, all the other formatting buttons are grayed out. There's no way back.

When the Holy Spirit gave the Corinthians faith in Christ's name (1 Cor. 6:11), their eyes turned from their irregular and uneven life-page to Christ's justified life-and-death page. As soon as they looked away from their unjustified page to his, his justified page became theirs. God viewed them as perfectly aligned with his law. Their story was changed by the StoryChanger because his Story became their story.

Remember, the Corinthians' biggest problem was their unrigh-teousness, but Paul climaxes this section on change by reminding them that their unrighteousness had been swapped out for Christ's righteousness.

Changing Our Story with God's Story

Praise Jesus the StoryChanger. If Jesus has revolutionized your story like this, praise him for this radical change, this total transformation! We may not have fallen into all these sins, but we all have dirty hearts that need to be washed, we are on the wrong side and need to be transferred, and we have an unjustified life story that needs to be justified. We all need inward change, even those who think they don't need outward change. We need to be justified by God, even if everything looks aligned to us or others. Remember, just one unjustified line means the page is unjustified. An unjustified line means an unjustified life. But even if every line comes up short, Jesus can align them all. Look from your page to his and praise him for giving you his page—actually his whole book—instead. What a rewrite!

Pursue change through Jesus's Story. Paul's basic argument was "Change your story because Jesus has changed your story." When it comes to petty disputes, use the power of forgiveness to empower forgiveness. Jesus has changed your past and your future, so be changed in the present. If you want to intensify the inner change and the positional change, understand that nothing multiplies change so much as changing your gaze from your life to Christ's. Our justification can never change, but its transforming power changes according to how much we keep it before us.

See more of your justification
to see more transformation.

Summary

Who can change our story from stuck to transformed, and how does that happen? *Rewrite your story now and forever by believing the Story-Changer's story.*

How God Changed My Story with His Story

I tried to change many times in my pre-StoryChanger life. I tried to live a cleaner life. I attempted to separate from sin and worked to get right with God. But my best efforts lasted only until the next temptation, when I would inevitably choose dirt and damnation instead. I sinned again and felt even more guilty and hopeless. Eventually I felt so guilty, so dirty, and so damned that I gave up even trying. I wanted to change, but there was no point. I could not change myself.

The StoryChanger changed all that. As I read the Bible, I came across story after story of change. As I listened to Christians talk and testify, I heard story after story of transformation. What made the difference? How could they change but I couldn't?

"Stop trying and start trusting." What? Did the preacher really say that? I pressed rewind on my car cassette player and listened to the old Baptist pastor say it again. "Stop trying and start trusting." He went on: "You're trying to change so God will accept you. You've got it all wrong. Trust God to accept you, and then he'll change you. Stop trying harder and start trusting harder." I just about wore out that minute of the tape in the weeks after, and I've replayed it in my mind almost every day since then. It's not *change, then you get Christ*; it's *Christ, then you get change*. It's not *try to change and then God will accept you*; it's *accept Christ and he'll change you*. Christ, then change; not change, then Christ. That changed my story forever.

Now when I'm tempted to sin, I say to myself, "Christ has changed me. I'm washed, sanctified, and justified. Christ has cleansed me, set me apart, and reformatted me. He's given me his Story to be my story, so I don't want to mess it up." When I see how perfect my new story is in God's eyes, I want to align my life with that. Strangely, trusting Christ for change makes me try harder to change.

Questions

1. How have you tried to change and what happened?

2. What's the worst sin and why?

3. Are you in the "Such am I" or the "Such was I" group? How do you get from the former to the latter?

4. By faith Christ's righteousness become ours. What happens to our unrighteousness (2 Cor. 5:21; 1 Pet. 3:18)?

5. Which of the three changes the Corinthians experienced are most influential in your life: washed, sanctified, or justified?

6. How can you increase the rate of change in your life?

Prayer

StoryChanger, you have changed my story with your Story, therefore help me to change by believing your Story. Amen.

What does this transformed life look like?
Let's read the first chapter of this new life.

Our stories will not change until we change the hero of our story. The StoryChanger changes our stories by making them all about him, not us.

6

The New Story

What's the most dangerous letter in the alphabet? Here's a clue: it's also the most dangerous letter in our lives. Need another clue? It's the thinnest letter in the alphabet. This makes it difficult to spot among other letters and hard to detect in our lives. So, what is it? The most dangerous letter in the alphabet is the letter *I*. Although it's the most popular letter in the world, it's the most dangerous letter in the world (and in our lives).

This thinnest of letters is the cause of our biggest problems and our sorest pains. There is no problem or pain in our lives or in the world that doesn't have *I* at the center of it. If we look at the worst chapters in our story, we'll find the letter *I* everywhere.

The greatest change the StoryChanger brings about in our lives is replacing the letter *I* with the letter *U*. Instead of pages covered in *I* he writes pages full of *U* (if you'll let me mix texting with my writing). Instead of our story being all about ourselves, it becomes all about others—two others in particular, as we'll shortly discover. What does a U-shaped life look like, and how do I get from a hideous *I* to a lovely *U*? Again, we get the answer from the apostle Paul, who went from living the most I-centered life to the most U-centered life. In Romans 15:1–7 he explains how the StoryChanger changes our story by breaking our ugly and suicidal *I* forever, gradually erasing its remains, and overwriting it with a beautiful life-giving *U*. Let's begin to beautify our lives today.

Background

Having explained the gospel of grace in Romans 1–11, Paul then outlines the life of grace in chapters 12–16. The gospel of grace broke the selfish *I* in pieces, and the life of grace erases its remains by writing a selfless *U* over it.

An area in which we see the U-principle at work is in how Christians relate to one another in secondary issues. In previous chapters, Paul had taught the Roman Christians doctrinal and ethical non-negotiables. But in chapters 14–15, he gives them guidance for other areas of life that aren't so much about truth or morals, but more about wisdom.

One of these areas pertained to food: should Christians follow Jewish dietary laws, and should Christians eat food that had previously been offered to idols? "Strong" believers had no hang-ups about ignoring Jewish dietary laws or about eating meat associated with idols. The "weak" were those who stuck rigidly to Jewish food laws and wouldn't touch food that had been offered to idols. This was dividing the Roman believers into opposing parties, with the strong being especially contemptuous and frustrated with the weak, and the weak being especially critical and condemning of the strong.

Although the food debate had no doctrinal or ethical consequences, the way the Romans reacted to it did. The main problem on both sides was an I-life instead of a U-life. Paul set out to change all of them into U-shaped lives. How did he do that? How do we get and grow a U-shaped life? In Romans 15:1–7 the apostle Paul connects our U-life with Christ's U-life. Christ's U-life is the model and fuel for our U-life. We'll therefore begin with a look at Christ's U-life.

How do I know what Christ's U-life looks like? Thankfully, we have his U-book to show us.

Christ Is a Perfect *U*

Three times Paul points to Jesus as our pattern of and propellant to a U-life. "*For Christ did not please himself,* but as it is written, 'The reproaches of those who reproached you fell on me.' . . . May the God of endurance and encouragement grant you to live in such harmony with one another, *in accord with Christ Jesus*. . . . Therefore welcome one another *as Christ has welcomed you*, for the glory of God" (Rom. 15:3, 5, 7). Let's take a closer look at these three parts of Christ's U-life and how they're relevant to the Roman situation and to ours.

Christ Worked at Pleasing Others

Here's one of the most astonishing statements in the whole Bible: "Christ did not please himself" (Rom. 15:3). Someone who never pleased himself? It's impossible for us to even imagine such an utterly selfless life. The vast majority of our lives are about pleasing ourselves. Almost every decision we make is determined by the question "What pleases me most?" But Christ never even asked this question. His pleasure, his preferences, his pride were never factors at play in his life. The only questions for him were "How do I please God?" and "How do I please others?" (in that order). His life was one big capital U with one arm of it reaching to God and the other to others. There was no *I* anywhere in his life. He laid down his life, his *I*, and, in doing so, became the foundational base for the two arms of U-shaped living.

With one arm he said to God, "Not my will, but yours, be done" (Luke 22:42), or, to put it positively, "I always do the things that are pleasing to him" (John. 8:29). With the other arm he said to others, "The Son of Man came not to be served but to serve, and to give his life as a ransom for many" (Matt. 20:28). Even when some of those he came to serve and save mocked and slandered him, he accepted it as part of the price to serve and save them (Ps. 69:9; Rom. 15:3).

Christ Worked for Unity with Others

Paul saw that Christ's peacemaking life was the only way to make peace among the Romans. "May the God of endurance and encouragement grant you to live in such harmony with one another, in accord with Christ Jesus, that together you may with one voice glorify the God and Father of our Lord Jesus Christ" (Rom. 15:5–6). Living in accord with Christ Jesus is living like Jesus lived. How did Jesus live? He lived for maximum harmony and minimal hatred. How did he do this? He did it by relying on his Father to give him endurance and encouragement.

Unifying God's people, and especially their voices, was hard and discouraging work. Left alone, they would splinter further apart and speak further apart. As we can see in the Gospel accounts of Jesus and his disciples, one of Jesus's top three tasks every day was harmonizing his disharmonious disciples. "Harmony . . . together . . . one voice" was not their default. But it was Christ's, and his Father gave him endurance and encouragement for the task.

Christ Worked to Welcome Others

One other area where Christ's U-life stood out was in the way he welcomed others who were different from him. "Therefore welcome one another as Christ has welcomed you, for the glory of God" (Rom. 15:7).

How did Christ welcome the Romans? He never visited the Roman church, therefore this is not speaking of bear hugs and holy kisses. It's referring to the way Jesus welcomed them through the gospel. Paul is saying, "Consider how different you were, Romans. Remember how unlike Christ you were. Recall how you disagreed with Christ and his gospel. And yet, through the gospel, Christ reached out to you with both arms to welcome you. He rolled out the red carpet to poor beggars."

Why did he do this? *For the glory of God.* He did this to make God more attractive and compelling. He did this because it burnished, magnified, and exalted God's character.

Changing Our Story with God's Story

Contrast your capital I. The Roman Christians were all about provoking, dividing, and rejecting. Like us, it is likely that they did not deliberately work at those behaviors. But such actions just happen when we don't work on pleasing, unifying, and welcoming as Christ did. When we see how ugly the Roman I-life was, let's ask God to show us how ugly our I-life is so that we start asking him for a U-life.

Worship the capital U. Christ's U-life was all about pleasing, unifying, and welcoming others. Let's pause and praise the perfect *U*. Delay with a doxology. Don't move on, but take some time to ponder and wonder at our astonishing Savior who imaged God so beautifully. He lived a perfect *U* in a totally *I* world.

For a good U-story,
read the best U-story.

How do I get from *I* to *U*? It seems a much
bigger chasm than twelve letters.

Christ Produces *I*'s

The Bible is a story of *I*'s becoming *U*'s. It was written to instruct us in many areas, but this is central: "Whatever was written in former days was written for our instruction, that through endurance and through the encouragement of the Scriptures we might have hope" (Rom. 15:4). The Bible encourages us and gives us hope that though we were created as *U*'s and deformed by sin into *I*'s, God's word can reshape us into *U*'s. By inviting us into his U-Story, God changes our I-stories into U-stories.

Reading the Bible's multiple I-to-U stories helps our story to change from *I* to *U*. The Bible instructs and changes us through history, songs, poems, prophecies, gospel accounts, and letters (see also 1 Cor. 10:6, 11). As Paul reminds the Roman believers, the Story-Changer produces *U*'s from *I*'s in four ways.

A New Compassion

"We who are strong have an obligation to bear with the failings of the weak, and not to please ourselves" (Rom. 15:1). Instead of impatient contempt for the weak, we show a patient kindness that puts them first and has compassion for them. Strength is given to us not to make *us* stronger, but to make the weak stronger. *Not* I *but* U.

A New Construction

"Let each of us please his neighbor for his good, to build him up" (Rom. 15:2). Instead of tearing people down for our pleasure, we build people up for their good. By our words and actions, we are builders not demolishers. Paul is not for sinful people-pleasing that aims at our own popularity, but holy people-pleasing that aims at others' good. *Not* I *but* U.

A New Cooperation

"May the God of endurance and encouragement grant you to live in such harmony with one another, in accord with Christ Jesus, that together you may with one voice glorify the God and Father of our Lord Jesus Christ" (Rom. 15:5–6). Instead of fighting one another, we love one another. Our lives are no longer like clashing cymbals, but a multipart harmony. Minor differences don't muffle our united doxology. *Not* I *but* U.

A New "Come on In"

"Therefore welcome one another as Christ has welcomed you" (Rom. 15:7). Did Christ wait until we agreed with him in every area before he welcomed us? No, he embraced us, if we simply had faith in him. When we consider whether we should reach out to others and warmly invite them to friendship, we don't ask first, "Will this please me?" but, "Will this glorify God?" Will this make God more attractive? *Not* I *but* U.

Changing Our Story with God's Story

Not I *but* U. Has your *I* been broken? Is it being gradually erased and overwritten with the two arms of a *U*? Are you reaching up with one arm to embrace Christ, and are you reaching out with another arm to serve others with the four C's? If not, read Christ's U-Story for a U-story. Read the Bible looking for I-to-U stories and praying that they would break and erase your *I* and grow and strengthen the two arms of your *U*. Remember, at the base of every *U* is Christ's life laid down for *I*'s who trust in him. Without that bowed-down and bowed-over body, no arms would grow from it.

U is a happier letter than I. If your pages are full of *I*'s, your life is full of tears. An I-life is a sad life. So how do you live a happier life? Start living it for others. Replace all the *I*'s with lots of *U*'s. I know that sounds like the worst kind of life, but try it, and you'll see it's actually the best possible life. The most miserable people are the most selfish people; but the happiest people I know are the most servant-hearted.

A self-service life is a sad life,
but a serve-others life is a happy life.

Summary

What does a new U-shaped life look like and how do I get from a hideous *I* to a lovely *U*? *Change your* I *to* U *with Christ's perfect* U.

How God Changed My Story with His Story

The hardest truth in the world to believe is that we are saved by Christ's grace not our works. The second-hardest truth to believe is that service is satisfying. At least, that was the case for me.

After swallowing grace and finding it so amazingly sweet, I choked on trying to swallow service. It was the antithesis of everything I'd ever believed and lived. I was a skinny, six-foot-three, complete capital *I*. There wasn't one atom of *U* in my body.

That didn't change completely when I met the StoryChanger, but he certainly put a big initial crack in my *I*. As time went on, my *I* continued to crumble, especially when I spent a year in Eastern Europe working alongside persecuted Christians who were helping other persecuted Christians. There I saw the most beautiful *U*'s I've ever seen, and realized how much *I* still remained in me. Seeing Christ's *U* in them weakened the devil's *I* in me. There's still much work to be done there. Sometimes I feel like I've only reached tadpole stage in my transformation. But these two tiny arms I now stretch out to Christ and others and find they bring me so much more happiness than serving myself ever did.

Questions

1. Where do you see *I* in your life?

2. Where do you see evidence that your I-life is in the past?

3. How will you practice the four *C*'s this week? What's your "four *C* plan"?

4. How can you show *U* instead of *I* in times of division and disagreement?

5. Give examples of Christ's U-shaped life in the Gospels.

6. Give examples of I-to-U changes in the Old and New Testaments.

Prayer

StoryChanger, I confess that my story is full of *I*'s. Use Christ's U-life and U-death to write me a new story full of U. Amen.

How can I be sure that the StoryChanger can change my story? We have many credible endorsers.

Credible influencers contribute to incredible change. A book with no reviews is a book without readers.

7

The Endorsements

What makes us buy a book? Publishers inform us that the most influential factors are the author, the title, the cover, and the endorsements.

We can all understand the appeal of a specific author, an interesting title, and an appealing cover design. But endorsements? What are they, and why are they important? Endorsements are the recommendations of the book by well-known experts. If we're hesitating over buying a book, an enthusiastic endorsement by someone we know or respect can increase our interest and confidence in the contents, tipping us over from browsers to buyers.

I've been trying to persuade you to trust the StoryChanger, Jesus Christ, to rewrite your story by inviting you into his. But does his Story have any endorsements? *Can we find reliable influencers who recommend the StoryChanger?* Can we find people whose stories have been changed for the better with the StoryChanger's story? Yes, multitudes, and we're going to hear from some of them in this chapter, beginning with David's endorsement in Psalm 66. Let's be open to powerful persuasion as we hear these transformative testimonials.

Background

All creation praises God in Psalm 65, and all people are invited to praise God in Psalm 66. The original singers of this psalm were praising God for a specific historical deliverance, but the psalm can be used to celebrate all stories of God's salvation.

Why did David commend God's Story? Because God has done great things in world history.

The Storychanger Changed World History

Psalm 66 begins by narrating the greatest Old Testament event in the past and propels us forward to an even greater New Testament event in the future.

The Greatest Old Testament Event

David called choirs to praise God loudly and joyfully (Ps. 66:1-4), because God redeemed Israel from Egyptian slavery, from the Red Sea, and into the Promised Land (66:5-12).

> Come and see what God has done:
>> he is awesome in his deeds toward the children of man.
>
> He turned the sea into dry land;
>> they passed through the river on foot.
>
> There did we rejoice in him. (66:5-6)

He reminded the choir of the harsh times Israel endured in Egypt, but also of how God brought them into the Promised Land.

> For you, O God, have tested us;
>> you have tried us as silver is tried.
>
> You brought us into the net;
>> you laid a crushing burden on our backs;
>
> you let men ride over our heads;

we went through fire and through water;
yet you have brought us out to a place of abundance.
(66:10–12)

David reminds Israel of how God massively changed their national story and, therefore, he commends this God as the one who can also change their present and future individual stories. This is great, but has God ever done anything greater than this?

The Greatest New Testament Event

Whenever we read a psalm, we should always ask ourselves, "How was this psalm fulfilled in the New Testament?" a practice Jesus engaged in (Luke 24:44). Psalm 66 was fulfilled in Christ's even greater redemption on the cross. There, Jesus defeated sin, death, Satan, and hell, and opened up the Promised Land of heaven to his people. At the foot of the cross, we celebrate the exodus redemption that Christ accomplished. There we say, as David did, "Come and see what God has done: / he is awesome in his deeds toward the children of man" (Ps. 66:5). At the cross, Christ transformed condemnation and death into salvation and life. His red cross is far brighter than the Red Sea.

Christ's story changed world history. He defeated hell, he atoned for sin, he rose from the dead, and he was rewarded with universal authority (Matt. 28:18). As great as the Old Testament story of redemption was, the New Testament one is even greater. Jesus changed the story of the world.

Changing Our Story with God's Story

World History. The Old Testament redemption (as seen in the exodus) changed Israel's history for the better. The New Testament redemption changed world history for the better. These two historical events are two historic endorsements of the StoryChanger's saving power. Do they persuade you to embrace Christ and endorse him yourself?

Wow History. God gave us historical events in both Testaments to recommend Christ to us. The Old Testament one was big, but the New Testament one was even bigger. Is our response to world-changing history "meh" or "wow"? Do we shrug our shoulders or lift our voices? The dry seabed is a persuasive endorsement, but the empty tomb is an even greater endorsement.

The empty tomb is
the fullest endorsement.

Jesus changed the world's story.
But can he change my story?

The Storychanger Changed David's History

A Personal Endorsement

After praising God in Psalm 66:1–4, David returns to praise again in verses 13–15. This time, though, it's not corporate praise but personal praise. It's not plural but singular, with five *I*'s and three *my*'s in these three verses. That personal praise climaxes in a personal testimony: "Come and hear, all you who fear God, / and I will tell what he has done for my soul" (66:16). He accepted God's invitation into God's Story and saw his own story rewritten. "Come and see Christ rewrite world history, then come and hear about how Christ rewrote my history."

A *Christ Endorsement*

What fueled David's endorsement? He refers to sacrifice multiple times in verses 13–15. Sacrifice was the way Old Testament believers expressed their faith in the coming Savior of sinners. Sacrifices did not save them from sin, but helped cultivate faith in someone whose sacrifice would. As David's physical eyes saw the sacrificial animal bleeding, dying, and burning, his faith-eyes saw Christ offering himself as a future sacrifice for sin. Christ's future Story changed David's story a thousand years before it was even written! No wonder David burst aloud with "Come and hear, all you who fear God, / and I will tell what he has done for my soul" (Ps. 66:16).

An *Unexpected Endorsement*

When trying to get endorsements for a book, authors and publishers reach out to influential and successful people. However, that's not how the StoryChanger works. He generally picks the weak, the unknown, and the failures! For example, remember adulterous, broken, abused, Ms. Samaria, whom we heard from in chapter 4? Jesus changed her story, and she endorsed him as the StoryChanger: "Come, see a man who told me all that I ever did. Can this be the Christ?" (John 4:29). David was far from perfect, but that made him a perfect endorser for the StoryChanger. The best endorsers of the StoryChanger are those whose stories he's changed. Though no publishers would ask for their endorsement, God does.

Diverse *Endorsements*

Publishers ask authors to seek endorsements from a range of people to appeal to a range of readers: men and women, old and young, pastors and missionaries, specialists and generalists. Similarly, each book of the Bible commends and endorses Jesus in different ways.

Genesis endorses Jesus as the *Creator*.
Exodus endorses Jesus as the *liberator*.
Leviticus endorses Jesus as the *sacrifice*.
Numbers endorses Jesus as the *guide*.

Deuteronomy endorses Jesus as the *covenanter*.

Joshua endorses Jesus as the *conqueror*.

Judges endorses Jesus as the *general*.

Ruth endorses Jesus as the *Redeemer*.

First and 2 Samuel endorse Jesus as the *Son of David*.

First and 2 Kings endorse Jesus as the *King of Israel*.

First and 2 Chronicles endorse Jesus as the *history-maker*.

Ezra endorses Jesus as the *church-reviver*.

Nehemiah endorses Jesus as the *church-builder*.

Esther endorses Jesus as the *protector*.

Job endorses Jesus as the *innocent sufferer*.

Psalms endorses Jesus as our *song*.

Proverbs endorses Jesus as *wisdom*.

Ecclesiastes endorses Jesus as the *satisfier*.

Song of Solomon endorses Jesus as the *lover*.

Isaiah endorses Jesus as the *suffering servant*.

Jeremiah endorses Jesus as the *new covenanter*.

Lamentations endorses Jesus as *new mercies*.

Ezekiel endorses Jesus as the *glory restorer*.

Daniel endorses Jesus as the *King of kings*.

Hosea endorses Jesus as the *backslider's friend*.

Joel endorses Jesus as the *Spirit-sender*.

Amos endorses Jesus as the *roaring lion*.

Obadiah endorses Jesus as the *deliverer from vengeance*.

Jonah endorses Jesus as the *missionary to Gentiles*.

Micah endorses Jesus as the *babe of Bethlehem*.

Nahum endorses Jesus as *slow-but-sure to anger*.

Habakkuk endorses Jesus as *mercy-rememberer*.

Zephaniah endorses Jesus as the *Lord of the day*.

Haggai endorses Jesus as the *desire of all nations*.

Zechariah endorses Jesus as the *fountain for the cleansing of sin*.

Malachi endorses Jesus as *angel of the covenant*.

Matthew endorses Jesus as the *promise keeper*.

Mark endorses Jesus as the *miracle worker*.

Luke endorses Jesus as the *great physician*.
John endorses Jesus as the *Son of God*.
Acts endorses Jesus as the *church's power*.
Romans endorses Jesus as the *justifier*.
First Corinthians endorses Jesus as the *uniter*.
Second Corinthians endorses Jesus as the *encourager*.
Galatians endorses Jesus as the *freedom fighter*.
Ephesians endorses Jesus as the *bridegroom*.
Philippians endorses Jesus as our *greatest joy*.
Colossians endorses Jesus as our *identity*.
First Thessalonians endorses Jesus as our *hope in death*.
Second Thessalonians endorses Jesus as the *devil-crusher*.
First Timothy endorses Jesus as the *church's mediator*.
Second Timothy endorses Jesus as the *church's guard*.
Titus endorses Jesus as the *church's organizer*.
Philemon endorses Jesus as the *slave's friend*.
Hebrews endorses Jesus as the *great high priest*.
James endorses Jesus as the *work producer*.
First Peter endorses Jesus as the *spotless lamb*.
Second Peter endorses Jesus as the *Judge*.
First John endorses Jesus as the *advocate*.
Second John endorses Jesus as *come-in-the-flesh*.
Third John endorses Jesus as the *proud parent*.
Jude endorses Jesus as our *fall-preventer*.
Revelation endorses Jesus as the *ultimate winner*.

Changing Our Story with God's Story

Be persuaded by these endorsements. God is persuading you
through these persuaders. How can you doubt his good will
toward you when you see how much he's put into persuading you, when he's sent so many persuaders to you? Do you

sense his desire to rewrite your story in these multiple and powerful endorsements?

Persuade others with your endorsement. If these endorsers have persuaded you, why not add your own endorsement? If Jesus has changed your story, why not commend him to others? Remember, if you don't commend Christ, he will condemn you (Luke 9:26). "But I'm not Moses or David or Matthew or Paul or John or the Samaritan woman. I'm just a nobody. How's my endorsement worth anything?" Every endorser thinks they're a nobody—otherwise God would not ask for their endorsement. Thankfully, God uses nobodies to tell everybody about the StoryChanger.

Use Christ's commendations,
or you'll have his condemnation.

Summary

Can we find reliable influencers who recommend the StoryChanger? *Use the biblical endorsements God has provided to move you from hesitation to transformation.*

How God Changed My Story with His Story

I hated school. I hated studying so much that I left high school one year early. The reasons were partly the disinterested teachers and partly the daily violence, but it was mainly myself. Apart from reading soccer magazines for the latest news about my idols and business magazines for the latest get-rich-quick schemes, I didn't read at all. I left high school without finishing a book.

Now I write about one book a year and endorse many books every year. What changed? I met an enthusiastic endorser early in my Christian life. When I sensed a call to the ministry, I had to work for a year before I could begin my six years of university and seminary education. During that year, I worked as a delivery driver for a friend who had his own printing business. As it was a new business with very few customers, we spent many hours every day in the shop where he enthusiastically fed this fledgling Christian multiple sermons, books, and Scripture memory verses.

His enthusiastic endorsement of Christ ignited my love of learning about Christ, and I hope this book can do the same for you. So, if I may add my own endorsement to those of the biblical authors, I'd say, "Jesus is my forgiver, my joy, my teacher, my guide, my rest, my love, my life, my joy, my all. I love endorsing Jesus, and pray I'm a living endorsement too."

Questions

1. What makes you hesitate to ask the StoryChanger to change your story?

2. What role have Christian testimonies played in your faith journey?

3. What was the role of sacrifice in the Old Testament (Heb. 9)?

4. Take the top ten books of the Bible you know best and come up with their endorsements of Christ, in your own words.

5. If you were asked to offer an endorsement of Christ, what would you say?

6. Who will you endorse Christ to this week?

Prayer

Thank you, StoryChanger, for these endorsements. Use them to move me from hesitation to transformation. Amen.

––––––––––

I believe Jesus can change my life story, but can he change my inside story? Let's see how reading Christ's narrative changes our inner narrative.

Our inner story becomes our outer story. A bad external story flows from a bad internal story.

8

The Inside Story

What story do you tell yourself about yourself? Whether we are aware of it or not, we all tell ourselves a story about ourselves. It may be a positive story or a negative story, but that inner story is often the most influential force in our lives. It's the first story we read every morning, changing the way we view the day and ourselves. It's the last story we read at night, affecting our sleep and our health. As Jim Loehr of the Human Performance Institute warned, "Since our destiny follows our stories, it's imperative that we do everything in our power to get our stories right."[1]

How do we do that? How do we find out if we're telling ourselves a bad story with bad effects? *And how do we change our inner story from a bad one to a good one and read it for the best results?* Joshua 1 helps us to identify our bad stories, replace them with good stories, and read those instead. The less we read our bad stories and the more we read good stories, the better and more enjoyable our stories will be, especially the endings.

---

1   James E. Loehr, *The Power of Story: Rewrite Your Destiny in Business and in Life* (New York: Free Press, 2007), 5.

Background

The book of Joshua is named after its principal character and narrates how he took over from Moses to lead the Israelites into the Promised Land. Through various promises and prophecies, God had given Joshua a wonderful story about the future to read and encourage him. However, it looks like Joshua was prone to read a story he made up himself, and read it so much that it became his own bad story.

What's the effect of reading a bad story?

A Bad Story Has Bad Effects

Joshua was at a turning point in his life. He'd been a faithful second-in-command, but now God was calling him to fill Moses's massive shoes. It would have been a daunting task for anyone, but it seemed to have been especially challenging for Joshua. Perhaps he was comfortable in his deputy or assistant role, but never saw himself as the leader, especially when his job description was "conquer Canaan." It seems that this was not a job Joshua wanted, and he'd already begun writing a terrible story about how bad it was going to be.

A Bad Story

What was Joshua's inner story? What was he thinking? Although it's not explicit in Joshua 1, his internal story is implied in God's repeated words to him, which likely addressed his present state of mind as well as prepared him for possible future challenges.

- Three times God told him to *be strong* (Josh. 1:6, 7, 9).
- Three times God told him to *be courageous* (Josh. 1:6, 7, 9).
- Three times God told him to *follow God's word* (Josh. 1:7, 8, 9).
- Three times God told him *he would be successful* (Josh. 1:6, 7, 8).
- Two times God told him that *he was with him* (Josh. 1:5, 9).

So, what story was Joshua telling himself? Its five parts correspond with God's five messages.

- Part 1: I'm weak.
- Part 2: I'm scared.
- Part 3: I don't know what to do.
- Part 4: I'm going to fail.
- Part 5: I'm all alone.

Try telling yourself that story every day. What do you think the effect will be?

Bad Effects

Obviously, such an internal story would have a negative impact on Joshua's mindset, his worldview, his feelings, his words, his decisions, and even his appearance and body language. He likely felt feeble, fearful, foolish, a failure, and forsaken. This was not good for him, and certainly not good for the two million people he was called to lead into battle.

Changing Our Story with God's Story

What's your inner story? Sometimes we hear and read our own inner story so much that we don't even realize we're doing it. We've gotten so used to our inner voice that we're not conscious of it anymore. But that story is there, and it's having an impact for good or for evil.

Jim Loehr has specialized in helping top performers identify the inner stories that are spoiling their life story. He's found that most people tell inner stories about five major subjects: work, family, health, happiness, and friendships.[2] I would add faith to this list. Further, I'd

2   Loehr, *Power of Story*, 5.

argue that what we believe about God, especially our relationship to him, influences us more than any other subject.

Loehr gets his clients to write out their inner story. That can take a few days and many rewrites. He then gets them to *title* their story, analyze the *text*, identify the dominant *theme*, hear the overall *tone*, and define the *target* (their life purpose or ultimate mission). What does your story look like using these five criteria? What's your *title*, *text*, *theme*, *tone*, and *target*? Once you see and hear the story you are reading and hearing most, you'll be able to decide whether it's true or not, and especially if its five parts align.

The best authors begin with the ending; they know how they want the story to end. Everything else is aligned with that and works toward it. So why not begin by asking yourself, What's my target? What's my life mission? How would I like to be remembered? What do I want written on my gravestone? Then look at how to align your title, text, theme, and tone with that target.

What's the impact of your story? Every story we read changes us to one degree or another, and none more so than our inner story, which we read and reread multiple times a day. Here are the titles of some of the inner stories people have told me in recent years. As you read them, imagine the impact of them on their readers: "I'm a cheap whore." "I'm fat." "I'm an imposter." "I'm a loser." "I'm unlovable." "I don't belong." "I'm a disappointment." What's the title of your book, and how is it impacting you?

A bad story
has a sad sequel.

How can my inner story change for the better
and therefore have better effects?

The Best Story Has the Best Effects

Having seen how bad inner stories can have such bad effects, how
do we get a better inner story with better effects?

God Tells Us a Better Story through His Word

God saw inside Joshua, heard his internal story, and replaced it
with a true five-part story corresponding to his false five-part
story.

- Part 1: *You will be strong.*
- Part 2: *You will be courageous.*
- Part 3: *You will follow my plan.*
- Part 4: *You will be successful.*
- Part 5: *You will have me with you.*

Can you imagine how God's Story changed Joshua's story? We
don't have to imagine, for we have a record of his conquest of
Canaan in the Bible. God's Story rewrote Joshua's story and rewrote history.

God Tells Us a Better Story through His People

God gave Joshua a new story to read, and then confirmed its five-
part message by the people's response to him (Josh. 1:16–18). Based
on their words, it seems that the people knew Joshua better than he
did. They could "hear" his inner story when they looked at Joshua
and heard his words. They therefore spoke God's Story into his life
in a life-changing way. In the next chapter, we'll explore further
how God uses the community of God's people to change our stories
with his Story.

Changing Our Story with God's Story

Be courageous. It takes a ton of courage to change the inner story we're reading. Even when it's damaging us, it's a story we're used to and have grown to accept. I imagine that Joshua's greatest courage wasn't taking on giant warriors but taking on the gigantic lies in his story. That battle for the millions of neural pathways in our brain is the most ferocious battle ever waged.

I have a friend whose dad physically and psychologically abused him. It devastated my friend's confidence and self-worth for decades. But later in life, when his dad tried to intimidate him again, this time with silence and facial expressions, my friend turned to his dad and said, "I will not let you terrorize me anymore." This not only led to freedom and a new sense of dignity for my friend, but it also began a new and healthier chapter in his relationship with his dad. Whoever wrote your inner story, if it wasn't God, you need to go to war to reclaim your brain and rewire it with God's Story.

Be convinced. You're not going to read God's Story unless you're convinced that you need it. So let me persuade you. Australian research found that "if churches do only one thing to help people . . . grow in their relationship with Christ . . . they would inspire, encourage, and equip their people to read and reflect on the Bible."[3] Similarly, the Center for Bible Engagement discovered that the number one thing you can do for yourself spiritually is read the Bible four times a week or more. Read it this frequently,

3   J. R. Briggs, "7 Ideas for Improving Bible Engagement in Your Church," *Christianity Today*, July 19, 2018, https://www.christianitytoday.com/.

and your life looks completely different to those who don't read the Bible, or read it less than that.[4] Another survey, which resulted in the book *Move: What 1000 Churches Reveal about Spiritual Growth*, found that "reflection on Scripture is, by far, the most influential personal spiritual practice."[5] Are you convinced yet?

Be consistent. If Bible reading is the best way to change our story with God's Story, then it's vitally important that we learn how to read it profitably. Here are some tips to help you read God's Story in a way that will change your inner story.

Small. Most Bible reading plans are too ambitious. I reckon only about 10 percent of people who start them continue with them for more than a month. If you can keep it up, great. If you can't, don't give up, but make it doable. Like every other exercise, short and often is better than big and rare. Five minutes a day every day will do you more good than thirty minutes whenever you can find time.

Same. Read at the same time and in the same place each day. Our bodies and minds love routine and rhythm. After doing something for twenty-five to thirty days, that practice becomes instinctive and a normal part of everyday life. Our

---

4 Arnold Cole and Pamela Caudill Ovwigho, "Bible Engagement as the Key to Spiritual Growth: A Research Synthesis," Center for Bible Engagement, August 2012, https://bttbfiles.com/web/docs/cbe/Research _Synthesis_Bible_Engagement_and_Spiritual_Growth_Aug2012.pdf.

5 Greg Hawkins, *Move: What 1,000 Churches Reveal about Spiritual Growth* (Grand Rapids, MI: Zondervan, 2011).

mind takes cues from the same time and environment to help get us into "Bible reading mode."

Simple. Keep it simple. Like physical exercise, we don't start with the hardest weights but with the easier ones. Start with a Gospel or with the Psalms rather than with Revelation or Leviticus.

Shut. Shut out distractions. Ninety percent of Christians find early morning is the best time for daily Bible reading (usually after a shower and coffee!) because that's the least distracting time. Turn off digital devices and don't let the internet steal your fresh mind. Write God's Story on your mind before the world writes its story there.

Study. Ask questions: How does this connect with my story? How does this rewrite my story? How can I share this story? If you're starting out or struggling, use a study Bible like the *ESV Study Bible* to help you understand God's Story without over-whelming you with extra reading. Or use the StoryChanger Devotional series to work through books of the Bible in just five minutes a day. Above all, pray for the greatest study help, the Holy Spirit, to write God's Story over your own.

Share. Write down one verse or one thought, or one idea from your reading. You could write it on an index card and carry that with you to look at when you eat or drink throughout the day. You can build a box of cards to reread at various points in the future. Also, why not ask a friend to read the same verses as you each day? Then you can connect and share your thoughts with each other as well as keep one another accountable.

Start. As Nike says, Just Do It!

Joshua's imperfect story of fear and our imperfect story of Bible reading remind us that our stories are far from perfect. That's why we need Jesus's perfect inner and outer Story to overwrite our imperfect inner and outer stories.

For a better story,
read the best Story.

Summary

How can our inner story change from a bad one to a good one? *Read the best Story for the best results.*

How God Changed My Story with His Story

I was abused in my childhood. I don't need to go into the details, as the perpetrators are long gone from my life. But the effects are not. Only recently did I realize how much that abuse had written a story deep into my psyche. Its many pages had one sentence on every line of every page: "You're nothing. You're nothing. You're nothing." What kind of effect did that awful story have? Not surprisingly, it caused terrible negativity, self-criticism, anger, shame, depression, and performancitis.

Performancitis? Yes, because I was so desperate to prove I was worth something, I worked way too hard and way too long in everything I did. Decades of striving, overwork, and perfectionism eventually damaged my physical and emotional health. But now that I've identified my inner story, I'm working every day to erase it and replace it with God's Story. God loves me, God chose me, God died for me, God saved me, God cares for me, God calls me, God communes with me, God lives with me, God desires me. God delights in me. God even sings songs over me (Zeph. 3:17). My status and identity are God-given, and no one can take that away. Instead of me believing "You're nothing," I now believe "I'm everything to God," and I don't need to do anything to prove that or preserve that.

Questions

1. "Our destiny follows our stories." Do you agree with this? Why or why not?

2. What's the title, text, theme, tone, and target of your story?

3. Which of these five aspects of your story are true or false? What parts are aligned or out of line? What do you need to change?

4. What parts of God's Story will you use to change your story?

5. What's your story about God and your relationship to him?

6. How will you get more of God's Story into your life and more of your own out of your life?

Prayer

StoryChanger, help me to read your Story most and my story least so that I can be changed for the better not the worse. Amen.

I need my external, internal, and eternal story changed. So, I've started reading the Bible, but I'm struggling to understand it. Where can I get help? That's where we need a book club.

Communal reading changes us more than personal reading. If we only read alone, we'll only change a little.

9

The Book Club

"Why should I go to church?" Even if you've never asked that question, you've probably been asked it by someone else.

The StoryChanger's reply is: "Because you'll hear a Story that will change the story of your life."

"But I can hear that Story online, sitting on the sofa in my pajamas, drinking coffee, and livestreaming church. God can change my story without my leaving my house. *Why should I go to church? What do I get out of it?*"

In Hebrews 10:23–25, the apostle Paul lists three benefits of going to a local church that we cannot enjoy when we are just a church of one.[1] Essentially, he says, if we want our stories to be rewritten, church must be part of the story.

Background

The Hebrew Christians were under pressure not to meet for church. As most of them came out of the Jewish church, joining the Christian church inevitably led to ostracism and even persecution. Understandably, some of them were asking, "Why go to church publicly with others when private church on my own is much safer?" That's a reasonable question. Can we give a reasonable answer?

---

1 Although Hebrews was written by an apostle, it's not explicitly stated to be Paul.

At Church We Confess Our Hope to One Another

God rewrites our story with his word. But he also rewrites our story with his people. He does this through his people sharing his word with one another. If you're unfamiliar with church, or if you need to view it through a new lens, why not look at it as something like a book club?

A book club is a group of people who gather regularly to discuss a book they're reading together. They usually meet at the same time and place each week or month. Usually someone leads the discussion, but the best groups are those where everyone participates. It's a good way to meet people, learn together, get questions answered, and keep one another accountable for reading the book. At times it may even lead to chatting with the author. (I've Zoomed into a number of book clubs that were reading one of my books to answer questions and take part in their discussions.) What do we get in God's book club?

We Get Hope

Paul connects churchgoing with hope-getting: "Let us hold fast the confession of our hope without wavering, for he who promised is faithful" (Heb. 10:23).

This world gets us down at times, doesn't it? We can feel hopeless about ourselves, our families, our job, and our country. How can we get hope? Paul says to the dejected, "Come to church to get an uplift of hope."

Our hope grows when we see others who've been hopeless and are now hopeful. Our hope rises when we see and hear people who've been through worse than us singing songs of joyful hope. Our hope develops when someone comes up to us after church, hugs us, and says, "I see you're a bit down today. Can I help?" Our hope matures when people tell us how God is helping them through a miscarriage by his faithful promises of heavenly hope for their little one. Our hope ripens when we see older believers still hoping in God without wavering even though they waver as they walk.

All these sights, sounds, and touches help me hold fast the confession of my hope without wavering, for he who promised is faithful.

We Give Hope

Sometimes our life goes so well that we can forget it's not going well for everyone else. We are flourishing and prospering in our families, work, or studies, making us self-satisfied and self-congratulatory.

Then we come to church, and we see people we would not usually see. We notice they weep during the prayer or have their head down during the singing. We see a harassed young mother trying to raise her kids and feeling like such a failure, wondering if she will ever not be tired again. We glimpse a man distracted during the preaching, someone who used to be super-engaged but now looks anxious and fearful. We catch sight of a young teen standing by herself, feeling lonely and unloved. We see so many people needing so much hope, and God brought us to church to help them recover hope with the faithful promises of God.

Church fills me with hope to fill others with hope.

"OK, I admit, more hope for me and others would be helpful. What else does church offer?"

At Church We Challenge One Another

"Let us consider how to stir up one another to love and good works" (Heb. 10:24). We've already considered one another. People have observed our hopelessness and helped us. We've noticed their hopelessness and helped them. But Paul asks us to go further, to spend some time thinking about how to challenge one another. "Why should I come to church?" Paul answers, "So that people can think about how to challenge you and so you can think about how to challenge others."

We Get Challenged

If you want to avoid being challenged, don't come to church. If you want to be just left alone, don't come to church. Some people's primary purpose is to challenge our souls, but they can't do that if they're in the pew and we're in the recliner.

We all need to be challenged. All of us default to slowing down and slouching our way along the Christian path. We cool in our love and zeal. Sometimes we can't see it ourselves, because we chill so slowly. That's why we need to be in the place where people can observe changes in our spiritual speed, health, energy, and activity, and spur us on.

We Give Challenges

But while accepting the challenge of others, we also want to be challengers of others. We don't do this out of retaliation; we do it out of love. Who can we challenge to follow Christ, serve Christ, be more like Christ, live more like Christ, and speak more of Christ? *How can we stir up someone to love and good works?* is a question that should be on our minds as we come and go from church. It takes a lot of thought to do this wisely and winningly. We don't just go around criticizing everyone else, but prayerfully ask God to show us someone to challenge and help us do it in a loving way that is clearly out for the person's good.

Church challenges me to be a challenger.

"But I don't need challenge. I need comfort." Come to church for that too.

At Church We Comfort One Another

Confessing our hope to one another and challenging one another can happen only if we're "not neglecting to meet together, as is the habit of some, but encouraging one another, and all the more as you see the Day drawing near" (Heb. 10:25).

We Get Encouragement

Sometimes we need to be challenged; other times we need to be comforted. Sometimes we need to be kicked out of bed; other times we need to be tucked in. Sometimes we need a poke in the eye; other times we need an arm round the shoulder.

We need that encouraging arm especially when we see "the Day drawing near." This may be the day of persecution, the day of death, or the day of the final judgment. Whatever it is, there are seasons when we need special spiritual encouragement.

We Give Encouragement

"Who can I encourage today?" That's a question we should ask God as we enter church. "Lord, show me those who need me to come alongside them and share what I've been reading in the Bible or something that blessed me in the sermon." This cannot be done via livestream or through books.

Church encourages me to be an encourager.

Changing Our Story with God's Story

Why should I come to church? I hope I have answered that question and not only persuaded you to come or keep coming but also helped you view church differently. It's the best book club in the world, not because it's attended by the best people in the world but because it's centered around the best book in the world by the best author in the world. There's a special promise given to those who gather together in this way. The author himself promises to be there in a special way (Matt. 18:19).

What should I do at church? Come to give and to get. To give and get hope, give and get challenge, and give and get comfort. Just as you would in any other book club, discuss the book with other book clubbers. Share your favorite verses. Talk about what impacted you the most. Ask questions about what puzzled you. Request accountability and give it too. Pray for people and ask people for prayer. There's so much you just cannot do without attending church in person. If we choose to livestream when we can be present, we turn what should be the most unselfish hour of the week into the most selfish. Yes, church can be uncomfortable.

It can be risky. It can be upsetting. But the sight, sound, touch, and sometimes even the smell of others are part of the Story that changes our story in ways we cannot imagine.

Summary

Why should I go to church? What do I get from church? *Use the confession, challenge, and comfort of church to rewrite your story and others' stories.*

How God Changed My Story with His Story

In my late teens, I would go to parties on Friday nights while my parents hosted the church youth group. Some winter nights I would get out of the cab I'd taken home to find that the youth group was still there. At two in the morning! It was a time of great spiritual interest in the church, and young people would gather with my parents for hours as they discussed the gospel and fellowshiped together.

Although this lively fellowship was a blessing for the church, I cursed these young Christians every time I was left standing outside in the cold. I couldn't go into my own house because Christians were there and I was looking and smelling like a devil. I would therefore spend the next hour or so walking round and round the block, waiting for their cars to leave so I could enter and go to bed. I was fuming. I hated Christians.

When I met the StoryChanger, I started to love those I had previously hated. I even enjoyed spending time with Christians. I loved sharing stories about the StoryChanger with them and hearing theirs too. I started loving going to church and being part of Christian fellowship. Instead of an angry cold heart, my heart now burns within me as I talk with Christ and his people along life's way.

Questions

1. In what other ways is church like a book club? In what ways is it different from a book club?

2. What other reasons would you give for why we should go to church?

3. What makes you lose hope? How would you help someone feeling hopeless?

4. In what ways do you need to be challenged and where do you need encouragement?

5. What are the benefits of in-person over online church?

6. Describe a time when someone's words at church made a big difference to you, or yours made a big difference to others.

Prayer

StoryChanger, thank you for giving me such an amazing book club. Use it to rewrite my story and other stories with your Story.

———

I love being changed by the StoryChanger. How do I change others with God's Story? We become storytellers.

If a story excites us, we're excited to share it. If a story bores us, we'll bury it.

10

The
Storytellers

One of the most popular podcasts in the world is *The Moth*. Dedicated to the art and craft of storytelling, *The Moth* also organizes various workshops and events to help people tell their stories without notes in a live stage performance.

It's called *The Moth* because its founder wanted to re-create the sultry summer evenings in Georgia when his friends would gather to tell tales to one another on the porch under a light, which attracted hundreds of fluttering moths. Now a worldwide organization, *The Moth* has presented over thirty thousand stories to standing-room-only crowds worldwide, and it produces more than five hundred live shows each year. The podcast is downloaded more than fifty million times a year, and *The Moth Radio Hour* is heard on over 480 radio stations worldwide.[1]

Clearly, people love to tell and hear stories, especially true and transformational stories drawn from life experiences. People listen to *The Moth* and attend the workshops because they hope the stories of others can change their own stories. In a way, it's like a secular church in which secular stories are shared among secular people for secular change.

1   *The Moth Radio Hour,* themoth.org/radio-hour.

But, as we've been learning, if we really want our lives changed for the better, we need to hear Jesus's Story. It doesn't stop there, however. If we've been changed by the StoryChanger, he calls us to be storytellers, just as he did with his first disciples, as we'll see shortly. This raises some questions: *What story are we to tell? Whom do we tell it to? How do we tell it?* We get answers to these questions in Matthew 28:18–20, where the StoryChanger commissions his Story-changed disciples to be storytellers.

Background

In chapter 7, we looked at multiple biblical endorsements of Jesus as the StoryChanger. We briefly noted that we are also called to be his endorsers. We can do this by telling how Jesus's Story changed our story. However, while there's an important role for telling our personal stories about the StoryChanger, we must never let our story displace the gospel Story. Our story has power, but Jesus's Story has greater power. Therefore, even when we are telling our story, we must use it to tell Jesus's Story.

How do we tell Jesus's Story? We begin by studying his Story.

We Study the Gospel Story

A Student of Jesus

Matthew had been a disciple (meaning "student" or "follower") of Jesus since Jesus had called him two or three years before (Matt. 9:9–13). Matthew's Gospel was his capstone project, his final thesis upon graduating from Christ's school. He had lived, heard, and seen the gospel Story for three years and was inspired by the Holy Spirit to record it and organize his notes into these twenty-eight beautiful chapters full of stories about the StoryChanger.

As he wrote about Christ's birth, life, death, and resurrection, Matthew presented Jesus as the fulfillment of Old Testament prophecy and the keeper of Old Testament promises. Jesus's Story was the most important Story in Matthew's life. Which explains why, apart from Matthew's call in Matthew 9:9–13, we actually find out very little about Matthew. His focus was Christ alone.

A Student of Sin

If we have no understanding of the story of our sin, then the Jesus Story has no relevance, power, or connection to us. We don't just study Jesus's Story and then by some magical, mystical process find that our stories are changed for the better. No, our stories are changed by the direct connection of Jesus's salvation Story with our sin story. We will never understand Jesus's Story or be changed by it for the better unless we read it through the lens of personal sin. If you reread the previous nine chapters of this book, you'll discover that each chapter helps us understand sin better so that we can understand salvation better. By seeing how sin changes us for the worse, we see more clearly how God's Story changes us for the better.

- Chapter 1: Sin messes up our lives into meaninglessness.
- Chapter 2: Sin ruins God's perfect world and plan.
- Chapter 3: Sin and Satan are the villains of our story.
- Chapter 4: Sin turns life into a desert.
- Chapter 5: Sin dirties us and damns us.
- Chapter 6: Sin mutates us into a big capital *I*.
- Chapter 7: Every book of the Bible points us from our sin to the Savior.
- Chapter 8: Sin damages us inside as well as outside.
- Chapter 9: Sin isolates us from Christ's school.

Sin makes Jesus's Story make sense, which is why Matthew studied sin as well as Jesus. Matthew began his Gospel with the name of Jesus, "for he will save his people from their sins" (Matt. 1:21). In chapter 2, he described how sin chased the infant Jesus around the Middle East. In chapter 3, we hear the first gospel sermon, preached by John the Baptist: "Repent, for the kingdom of heaven is at hand" (3:2). In the first public event of Christ's ministry, Jesus's baptism depicted his mission to cleanse us from sin (3:13–17). In chapter 4, Jesus triumphed over temptation to sin (4:1–11), described his mission as light dawning in a sin-darkened world (4:12–16), and preached his first gospel sermon, using the same "repentance" text as John did (4:17). We could go on and on. At every point, Matthew is studying sin and the Savior, and the more he learns about the one, the more he learns about the other.

Changing Our Story with God's Story

Study your sin story. Ask God to help you to see your sin more and more so you can see the Savior more and more. Ask for the Holy Spirit's assistance in both of these studies, because his two main gifts are showing us our sin (John 16:8) and showing us Jesus (16:14). We understand Jesus's Story better when we understand our sin better (and vice versa).

Study the Savior's Story. We need daily contact with the StoryChanger's Story if we want daily deliverance from sin and growing likeness to Jesus.

Our Savior shows us our sin,
and our sin shows us our Savior.

We've heard our sin story and the Savior's Story.
What do we do with it now?

We Speak the Gospel Story

After the disciples had studied under Jesus for three years, he sent them out to recruit more students. What they had heard, they were to tell. They had heard Jesus's Story, and they were to tell Jesus's

Story. But how are we to do that? Hearing the Story is easy; telling the Story is hard. That's why Jesus's last lesson was some basic training on storytelling, which we can sum up in five words.

Compulsory

Gospel storytelling wasn't optional for Jesus's disciples; it was required. Jesus doesn't make a tentative suggestion here; he issues an authoritative command. That's why he prefaces his command with an assertion of his universal authority: "All authority in heaven and on earth has been given to me" (Matt. 28:18). He had earned the title of Supreme Sovereign of heaven and earth by his gospel work, giving him a gospel authority to commission his students to be storytellers.

Comprehensive

"Go therefore and make disciples of all nations" (Matt. 28:19). Christ's commission was not local and limited but international and unlimited. Jesus instructed the disciples to make the world their classroom. Although they were only taught in Galilee, they were now to teach the globe. Christ called them to come and learn of him (Matt. 11:28), but then go and live for him. There must be an element of "going" in every Christian life. "Going" involves moving out of our comfort zone and into the discomfort zone. Although some will do it more than others, and some will do it better than others, all Christians do this to some degree.

Community

They weren't just to teach disciples; they were also to baptize them: "baptizing them in the name of the Father and of the Son and of the Holy Spirit" (Matt. 28:19). The mention of baptism reminds us that the majority of this learning and teaching is to be done under the auspices of the church. The local church is to be at the center of all evangelism—training evangelists and doing evangelism.

We invite others into a community of fellow disciples. But we also invite others into the community of God. Baptizing in the name of the three persons of the Godhead means that students are invited into community with God himself in the fullness of his three persons.

Consistent

Jesus's instructions are simple: "teaching them to observe all that I have commanded you" (Matt. 28:20). Tell the Story you heard. Teach the students what Jesus taught you. It's to be Christ's curriculum, not ours or anyone else's (2 Tim. 2:2).

Confidence

First-time speakers at *The Moth* usually describe the incredible sense of loneliness when they stand on stage for the first time. There is a single spotlight, and no one else is in it but the storyteller. TED speakers say the same about the famous red dot being the loneliest place in the world. But when we tell Jesus's story, we're guaranteed that Jesus is with us in a unique way: "And behold, I am with you always, to the end of the age" (Matt. 28:20). We're never alone when we're telling his Story.

Changing Our Story with God's Story

Tell the complete Story with complete confidence. When missionary David Livingstone was facing almost certain death at the hands of hostile tribes in Africa, he wrote in his diary: "January 14, 1856. Evening. Felt much turmoil of spirit in prospect of having all my plans for the welfare of this great region and this teeming population knocked on the head by savages tomorrow. But I read that Jesus said: 'All power is given unto Me in heaven and in earth. Go ye therefore, and teach all nations, and lo, I am with you alway, even unto the end of the world.' It is the word of a gentleman of the most strict and sacred honour, so there's an end of it! Should such a man as I flee? I feel quite calm now, thank God!"[2]

2 F. W. Boreham, *Texts That Made History* (New York: Abingdon Press, 1920), 129.

Later that year, Livingstone received an honorary doctorate from Glasgow University. As he rose to receive his degree, a hush descended. African diseases had withered his body, his lion-savaged arm hung disabled by his side. He stunned the crowd by announcing his intention to return to Africa: "'But I return,' he says, 'without misgiving and with great gladness. For would you like me to tell you what supported me through all the years of exile among people whose language I could not understand, and whose attitude towards me was always uncertain and often hostile? It was this: "Lo, I am with you alway, even unto the end of the world!" On those words I staked everything, and they never failed!'"[3]

They'll never fail us either.

Practice and pray. Don't let the gospel Story be the greatest story never told. Practice the Story and pray for storytelling opportunities in everyday life. Practice and pray, practice and pray. Tell the gospel Story to yourself in everyday life situations. If you connect it to your own life, then you'll be able to connect it to other people's lives. Tell the StoryChanger's Story, and watch him change lives through your storytelling. What a privilege and joy it is to be used in this way. Can you think of anything better than being a storyteller for the StoryChanger? The StoryChanger uses storytellers as storychangers.

Be the story. "But I'm such a poor speaker. I get all tongue-tied and confused." Here's the good news. We may not be able to speak the gospel but we can be the gospel. Paul said to Christians just like you in Corinth, "You yourselves are

---

3 Paul Rees, introduction to C. Peter Wagner, *Defeat of the Bird God* (Grand Rapids, MI: Zondervan, 1967).

our letter of recommendation, written on our hearts, to be known and read by all. And you show that you are a letter from Christ delivered by us, written not with ink but with the Spirit of the living God, not on tablets of stone but on tablets of human hearts" (2 Cor. 3:2–3). Paul encouraged them to show if they couldn't tell, to live the gospel and therefore communicate it by acts and attitude. Changed stories change stories. But people will ask you, "What's changed?" So let's always be ready to tell our story of the StoryChanger even if we don't get every word right.

Storytelling is story-changing,
and story-changing is storytelling.

Summary

What story are we to tell? Who do we tell it to? And how do we tell it? *Tell the complete gospel Story to everyone with clarity, consistency, confidence, and charity, and the StoryChanger will change others' stories.*

How God Changed My Story with His Story

I must confess that I'm not a good one-on-one storyteller. Sure, I can preach, podcast, and write the StoryChanger's Story. But I still struggle when it's just me and my neighbor, or just me and my barber, or just me and someone beside me on the plane. It's a part of my story that still needs a lot of rewriting. My "private storytelling chapter" is way too short and has way too few happy endings.

The two parts of God's Story that are helping me to change my story in the area of private storytelling are this Great Commission in Matthew 28 and these words from Paul: "For I am not ashamed of the gospel, for it is the power of God for salvation to everyone who believes" (Rom. 1:16). Or, to paraphrase, "I am not ashamed of God's Story because it is the power of God to change my story and that of everyone else who hears and believes it too."

Questions

1. In what ways do you study Jesus's Story? How could you become a better student?

2. How do we decide when to tell the gospel Story of Jesus and when to tell our story of Jesus?

3. How has studying sin helped you learn more about Jesus?

4. Which of the five words about storytelling challenge you most (*compulsory, comprehensive, community, consistent, confidence*)?

5. Practice explaining the gospel Story to someone in one minute.

6. How can you become a better storyteller?

Prayer

StoryChanger, help me to tell the whole gospel to the whole world with Christlike clarity, consistency, and confidence. Amen.

Is that the end of the story?
In a way, it's just the beginning.

The End

You've realized your story must be rewritten, you've asked the Story-Changer to change your story, your story has already begun to change, and you've begun to change other stories with God's Story. What's next? What happens at the end of your story?

Eternal Story

Our stories will end in this world, and the world's story will end eventually too. However, that's not the end of God's Story. In fact, our story and the world's story are just the introduction to endless chapters of God's eternal Story. God has written a heavenly, perfect story for us that will start the moment our story in this world ends. It's a story that will never end, and it will be so good we'll never want it to end.

Happy Story

That's not the end of change though. The StoryChanger will continue to change our story in heaven. That change is not from condemnation to salvation, or from sin to holiness, or from weakness to power. It's from glory to glory, from grace to grace, and from one degree of perfection to another.

There, we'll increasingly understand our past story and the world's story. We'll hear others' stories and grow in our appreciation of how these stories interacted with ours and with God's. We'll hear Jesus's Story as we learn more and more about his character, his person, and his work. We'll never run out of stories to tell, hear, or enjoy. Every story will be a happy story, and we'll never hear a sad one. The story-shredder will be shredded forever in hell, together with those who rejected the StoryChanger and chose to stick with their messy and meaningless stories.

Changed Story?

Which raises the question: Have you turned your story over to the StoryChanger and asked him to rewrite your story? Or are you still the author of your own story, trying to write some happy chapters and hoping for a happy ending? Remember, your story here in time will determine your story in eternity. You won't get a second chance; you won't get a rewrite. Can you not see how much you need the StoryChanger and how willing he is to change your story with his? I'm pleading with you to stop typing, press delete by confession, and hand your keyboard to God by faith. Ask him to rewrite your story by inviting you into his.

Perfect Story

If you do, the end of this book will mark the beginning of your new book, your rewritten story. God will immediately give you Jesus's perfect Story as your own. Yes, that's right: when you give Jesus your faith, he gives you his Story (2 Cor. 5:21). We can then come to God in Jesus's name, and God will treat us as if we were Jesus and had lived Jesus's life. Do you know how loved that makes us (John 17:23)?

The more we realize how perfectly loved and accepted we are by God, the more we will want our story in this world to match Jesus's perfect Story. So how do we do that? How do we keep changing our story on earth with Jesus's Story?

Shared Story

To continue and accelerate that change, I invite you to join me and other StoryChangers at *thestorychanger.life*, where we share God's Story and stories of how God has changed our lives with his Story. You'll also find daily devotionals to sustain change and advance it. You'll hear interviews with those whose stories have been changed by God's Story. And you'll get help with telling God's Story so that you become a storychanger for the StoryChanger. I look forward to seeing you there and together changing stories with God's Story.

Scripture Index

The StoryChanger Devotional Series

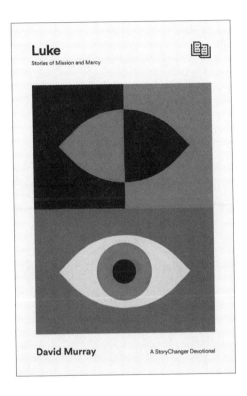

When people know God's story better, their own stories change for the better too. This devotional is a friendly, practical guide to understanding Scripture and how it shapes your story.

This volume features daily readings designed to help you learn, love, and live the whole Bible. David Murray walks through the Gospel of Luke, offering thoughtful expositional comments on the book's message, reflection questions, and a personal pray to think through each day. This series can help you reorien' your mind and transform your life with God's better stor'

For more information, visit **crossw'**